The Simple SuperMom

Easy, Practical Tips and Hacks for Saving Time, Money, and Your Sanity

by Kelly Stewart

Copyright © 2022 All rights reserved.

OVERVIEW

Part I: Saving time and money

- Chapter 1: Money, Minutes and Munchies – How to Save on Groceries and Cooking
- Chapter 2: Feeding the Masses – Meal planning (Don't skip this one!)
- Chapter 3: The Dreaded Tasks – Cleaning & Laundry
- Chapter 4: So Much Stuff!!! – Decluttering & Organizing
- Chapter 5: Kickin' You-Know-What – Productivity tips
- Chapter 6: More Ways to Spend Less – Simple budgeting tips

Part II: The Icing on Top

- Chapter 7: Five Minutes Counts
- Chapter 8: Simply Special – Easy Ways to Make Things Special
- Chapter 9: Big or Small, More or Less? – Simple Decorating Tips
- Chapter 10: Help Them Help You – Simple Parenting Hacks
- Chapter 11: Everything but the Kitchen Sink – Miscellaneous tips

Introduction

Okay, let's just get this out of the way right now. Before you get worried about the word "SuperMom" in the title, let me reassure you. This is NOT a book that is designed to make you feel like you need to be the "Perfect Pinterest Mom." No one is perfect, period. (If you ask my family, I'm sure they will quickly volunteer a whole spectrum of examples of just how far from perfect I am!) Point being, we're all human – we make mistakes, we have quirks, and we each have a hard time dealing with certain things. We're also usually our own worst critic. No one should be striving to be THE perfect (fill in the blank) anything – it's an illusion that will leave you feeling lacking and less than, and that's the exact opposite of what I want for you and what you deserve.

So nope, no perfection here. Perfection is not the goal – easy improvement is. I'm sure you've heard it before, but I want you to really take this phrase to heart: progress over perfection. Such a simple phrase, but one that is SO true – and often so hard to keep in mind while we're self-critiquing. We're not aiming for perfection. We're not aiming for making your home more impressive or company-worthy either – both of those "standards" are based on other people's opinions of your home or your life. Nope, this is about YOU – *I* don't care how you handle your laundry or organize your cabinets or whether you meal prep, and neither should anyone else who doesn't live in your home. Are you friends with your bestie because she keeps her floors clean enough to eat off of? Of course not, because that's not *your* home or your life. (And no, this book isn't aimed at convincing you to keep a sterile, spotless house either.) Lord knows that's obviously not why any of *my* friends have hung around!

What is this book for then? It's designed to help you improve your everyday, in the simplest ways possible – so you can know that you're living as the best version of YOU and giving the best of yourself to YOUR life, but without feeling like you're striving for an impossible goal or making your life more complicated. No ma'am, we're going for SIMPLE. This is all about practical tips and tricks that are easy to implement and can simplify or streamline every area of your life to make it run more efficiently - so that you can save more of your precious time, hard-earned money, and (perhaps most importantly, especially for moms) your SANITY.

Ever had one of those venting session with a friend – you know, the ones where you're talking over coffee (or Facebook, or over the sound of kids squealing) and commiserating over the daily/weekly struggles that make you want to pull your hair out? How do this many people make this many dirty dishes? Why is the laundry pile never-ending? How does my house look like a disaster area again thirty minutes after I just cleaned it? When does it ever end?!? Yeah, that kind of chat. Well, think of this book like one of those chats with your best friend, where y'all really get deep into things – except instead of only venting and agreeing with each other, you *also* brainstorm ways to actually

FIX the things that are causing you stress! That's what this book is. This isn't a scholarly book (although I swear, I do actually know how to use proper grammar). It's a chatting-with-your-girlfriends book. It's talking with another mom who's been there and wants to help you! It's here to give you motivation and some specific tips that can help you make changes that ultimately result in less daily stress for YOU in your home. I'm not an expert, but I AM proof that things (and people) can change and get better. There is no prize for being the "busiest" or the most stressed, despite how our society often seems to exalt these – as if *not* being "too busy" or stressed must mean you're not doing enough. I'm calling BS on that. There is absolutely nothing commendable about running yourself ragged, making things harder on yourself, and feeling like a frazzled failure – especially if you just end up looking around and feeling like others are doing such a better job at life than you are, and you wonder why you can't measure up.

Spoiler alert: Want to know WHY you never seem to measure up to the women who seem like they have it all together? It is NOT because they're out there kicking butt while you're just falling on yours. It's because you're measuring your real life against the thumbnail-size, photoshopped snapshot of theirs. You don't see their "behind the scenes", their failures, their habits and routines (both good and bad), etc. – you're comparing their polished, public surface to the minute-by-minute mess of your everyday. Trust me, they're not any closer to perfection than you are. Ever seen those side-by-side comparisons of what celebrities look like without their professionally done makeup on? Exactly. You're only seeing your friend's televised finished product, not the 27 takes that it took her to get there. Comparing ourselves to others is unfortunately human nature – which is why, more than likely, she feels the same as you and thinks that SHE is the one who's lacking and falling behind. Luckily, you're both wrong. Each of our journeys and our lives is different. Each of us excels in different areas, cares more about certain things, and couldn't care less about others. There ARE some tips and habits though that can help each of us get a better grip on feeling like we're happily and confidently in control of our life and how it functions. That's what I'm here to help with!

Let's be clear though. I'm here to help with all that NOT because I'm an expert, but because *I've been there!* I know how it is to feel like your life is running you (not the other way around). I've experienced the anxiety-inducing overwhelm that can come from your home being cluttered, messy and out-of-control. I've definitely been in the situation of standing exhausted at the end of the day, looking around you at a house that looks like it hasn't been cleaned or picked up in a month (even though you feel like you cleaned it 5 times just today), and feeling defeated because you feel like you've been spinning your wheels all day and have nothing to show for it. I've felt the resentment and frustration that can so easily build when you're tired and feeling overwhelmed and it seems like you're the only person in the home who's trying to keep up with things while everyone else works against you. One step forward and three steps back. I HAVE BEEN THERE – and I want to help make sure that you never experience that (or never again). This book isn't going to help you become a world-renowned 5-star chef. It's not a "how to become a quick millionaire" guide (there already seem to be plenty of those). I'm also not suggesting that once you read this book, you'll magically morph into a perfect combination of Martha Stewart, Betty Crocker, Betty White, and Super Nanny. This is not an "everyone needs to do things exactly this way" guide – our society doesn't need perfect Stepford Pinterest Wives. At the end of the day, YOU know your life best. I obviously don't know all the specifics to your life, your family, your schedule, etc. Your life is unique to you, and you have to make the ultimate decisions on what makes the most sense for YOUR life. My purpose is to help show you that it's possible and easier than you imagined to live that life in a way that makes you feel content and proud every day, with less stress involved to get there.

While I may not know details of the problems or challenges that are specific to you, I do know that there are suggestions in here that will help anyone. We're going to walk through simple, practical steps that will help you work better FOR yourself, instead of against. These chapters are bursting full of suggestions and tips that you can begin implementing right away that will give you immediate (but more importantly LONG TERM) results. If there are other family members living at home with you, we're also going to discuss simple ways to help them live in a way that helps the whole family (and you). Improving your habits and "leveling up" in areas that you may feel lost in or stressed about doesn't have to be complicated though (in fact, there are numerous tips in here that will help you in 5 minutes or less)! I've tried the complicated methods, and most of them simply weren't worth it to me. There's a wide variety of suggestions and examples in here because across the board we women have many different life situations, each one as unique as we are.

Regardless of the uniqueness of our circumstances though, we can all benefit from some added simplicity and peace in our lives. And THAT, my friend, is what you're going to get. Throughout the book, we'll talk about several different "versions" of you – Current You (you're sitting here reading this book right now), Future You (that could be you tomorrow, next week, or months from now), Morning You (the version of you that gets up every morning, depending on whether you're a morning person or not), and Evening You (you guessed it – the "you" right before bedtime). They're all part of YOU, but they may not be working well as a team. We're going to change that – so a large portion of this book is geared toward tips and habits that Current You can implement (with very little effort) in order to make things easier and less stressful for Future You. The majority of the suggestions and tips mentioned take VERY little time to do (some as little as 30 seconds), but they'll have lasting positive effects on the daily flow of your home and your life. A few may be a little more labor-intensive up front (and I'll point that out), but I promise that they're worth more than their weight in gold for the impact that they can have.

Not every suggestion in here will work for you, and that's exactly as it should be! You know your life and family best, so you can pick and choose which ideas to use to make your life run smoother — and leave the rest here. I want to help you set yourself up for success, so that each day feels like a smooth ride with as few bumps as possible. Perfection isn't attainable – but feeling like you finally have the "insider secrets" that allow you to go through each day and feel like you "have it all together" just like those women you've envied IS! It's not rocket science – these are just practical, uncomplicated habits and routines that will help you feel like a SuperMom, simply. You don't even have to be a mom; most of what's discussed here will help you regardless of whether you're married or not, have kids (regardless of their ages) or not, or work outside the home or not. Anyone can benefit from being able to both simplify and level-up their life at the same time.

If you want to absorb all the helpful ideas you possibly can in all the areas we're going to cover, then forge ahead – cover to cover. If you know there's a certain area that's currently stressing you out the most though, feel free to flip to that section first and then you can go back and read the rest. Either way, you're going to find TONS of great tips in here for making your life easier in many ways. Some of them may be things you already do – that's awesome! Some won't be applicable to your current circumstances – that's fine. Many of them though are likely to make you get excited and repeatedly exclaim to yourself "Yes! I'm going to try that! And that one! Ooh, and this one too!" That's why I wrote this! Don't overwhelm yourself though. Trying to start too many new habits or routines at once is a recipe for self-sabotage and disappointment. Instead, tab some pages and highlight the tips you want to try first; or keep a pen and a notepad or some post-it notes handy (or use a note app on your phone) to jot down ideas or page numbers that stand out to you the most. This way you'll have your own shorthand guide to look at in the coming weeks so you can remember the tips you wanted to implement first. Then you can come back to sections again later and refresh your memory on additional habits or changes that you want to add in – and repeat as needed until any chaos, stress and overwhelm that you feel right now is only a distant memory.

Oh, and if we're just meeting, I'm Kelly. I'm a working mom, my house is not spotless, I keep some frozen pizzas in my freezer, I would willingly procrastinate changing the litter box for weeks on end if there weren't dire smelly consequences, and I once accidentally made eggs explode and plaster *every square inch* of our kitchen with sprayed-on scrambled egg texture. I also weirdly enjoy organizing stuff, get rejuvenated by spending time chatting with other mom friends, and I absolutely love helping friends out however I can. So, you've come to a safe place and I'm so happy you're here. We're friends now, so grab your cup and let's chat!

Part I:
Saving Time and Money

Chapter 1: Money, Minutes and Munchies – How to Save on Groceries and Cooking

There's a reason we're starting here, with food (and it's not just because I love to eat). Regardless of how many people live in your household and whether or not you work outside the home, this is an area of your life that you have to deal with every single day. Not only can it take up a significant portion of your time (if you let it), but it can also easily be one of the largest expenditures each month in your budget. It's time to get excited about this though – because it's also an area in your budget where you have the most control and can make the biggest impact on saving your money!

First, we're going to cover a bunch of helpful tips and ideas to save money on your groceries while still being able to have delicious, nutritious food (my fave kind). I'll also talk about simple methods you can use to save time (and even some extra money) while cooking so that you don't feel like you're always stuck in the kitchen! Then in the next chapter, we'll expand on these and look at how meal planning can help you save even MORE time and money (without having to eat the same boring stuff every day). If the mention of "meal planning" just made you cringe though, don't worry! We're focusing on SIMPLE ways to improve your life, remember? There may be a few that aren't as simple as the rest, but this is a "pick and choose" collection anyway (or as some would call it, a "spaghetti method" – throw it all at the wall and see what sticks)!

Before we look at meal planning or even cooking though, let's start with ways to save money and time on buying groceries in the first place.

Groceries...

Before you go... Let's start with some tips to keep in mind before you even head to the store (or click to make an online grocery order). Aside from the entire next chapter (which will almost exclusively come into play before you get your groceries), there are some pointers that can help you save money even if you don't meal plan. First, you'll need to "shop" at your own house first. Check your pantry, freezer, and refrigerator to see what items you already have on hand and don't need to buy more of; also make sure to check your list twice by looking at these areas again AFTER you've made your grocery list, just to be sure you didn't include anything that you don't actually need to buy. This is just one of the reasons that it can be helpful to keep "like items" grouped together in your pantry and freezer (meats all together, frozen vegetables together, breakfast items, etc.) – this makes it much simpler to see what you already have and what you need, not to mention making it easier to find the item you're looking for when it's time to cook! Next, you can start by looking at the weekly sales ads for your local stores. See what "big ticket items" (meats, proteins, dairy, etc.) are on sale and start your list with those!

If you are hyper-focused on saving grocery money, try making your own price "cheat sheet" for your most-used items. Make a list on your phone (or on paper, but most of us keep our phone on us all the time) of your most commonly purchased grocery and household items and list what they normally cost at the stores you frequent. This way when you're out shopping (especially if it's at a store you're not in frequently), you won't have to wonder whether a "sale" is actually a good deal on that particular item, or if the sale price at that store is still more than what you normally pay for the product at another store. This also helps you know whether it's a good enough deal to want to stock up on extras of the item to save for later! Since inflation is affecting grocery prices in much of the US right now, this list can also come in handy if you're out shopping and are curious on how much an item's price has gone up since the last time you purchased it. (This might make you rethink a few of the items on your shopping list!)

Do you have a habit of seeing what seems like a good deal on an item at the store, and you can't remember how many of that item you have at home or whether you need more, so you just go ahead and buy some – only to later get home and realize you already had more than enough on hand, and now wish you hadn't spent the money on them? Try this then – before you head to the store, use your phone to take a few quick pictures or video of what's in your pantry and freezer (you're more likely to remember what you do/don't have in your fridge since you look in it the most). This way, if you see a deal on something at the store that wasn't on your list but you think you MIGHT need some, you can easily pull up the pics/video you took and see what you actually already have in stock at home.

Okay, now you're almost ready to head to the store. The last thing to consider before you go is… Don't! Don't go. [What?!?] Statistically, the less often that you grocery shop then the more money you save overall. It's pretty basic, but true – if you're not shopping, you're not spending money. So, before you decide to run to the store for "just a couple of things," look at whether there's a way for you to wait another few days (or even longer) and make some ingredient substitutions to avoid getting into the store and dealing with the temptation of "well, while I'm here I'll just grab this too…and this…and that…" See what I mean?

Now once you walk into the store, head to their usual spots for clearance food items first. Often there may be seasonal or holiday-themed pantry items on clearance that still have a long shelf life left (I got boxes of delicious Christmas brownie mix for 75% off in February, even though they didn't expire until the *next* Christmas). Most grocery stores will also have certain spots where they put bakery items that are on clearance and meat or dairy items that have been marked down. The bakery/meat/dairy items are generally marked down because they are at the end of their shelf life, but don't ignore these – chances are most of them can be put in your freezer (if you wouldn't use them right away) and stay good for months to come! If it's at item that you're going to immediately freeze and it's near the end of its shelf life, leave the "clearance" sticker on it (or add one yourself if it doesn't have one on each package) – this will be a reminder to you when you pull it out of the freezer later that it needs to be used as soon as it thaws (and not left in your fridge for a few days before you get around to cooking it).

As you continue down your list and go through the store, pay attention to the price per ounce/unit so that you can get the most "bang for your buck" (which does not always mean getting the largest size). While a large bulk container of something often equates to the best price per unit/weight, it's always best to check to be sure. This includes paying attention to the price per weight/unit for vegetables and comparing prices for fresh, frozen, and canned ones to find the best deal. Speaking of vegetables (and other produce), another way to save money is to buy whole produce and then cut it up yourself; don't pay extra for the small convenience of having it already sliced/diced. This concept applies to snack foods and lunch items as well – try to avoid paying extra for ones that are individually packaged if you can, and instead buy larger containers/bags of the food and portion it out yourself at home into small snack baggies. Pretzels, goldfish or cheese crackers, animal cookies, and other food items can all be purchased and sorted at home this way. You can often find better prices on cheese if you buy it as a block and then shred it at home, rather than buying bags of pre-shredded cheese (plus the pre-shredded kind doesn't melt as well in many recipes). Even things like applesauce and yogurt can be purchased in larger tubs and then put into smaller reusable containers at home to pack into lunches for the week. Do this at the beginning of the week and not only do you save money (since you get more "food for your buck" by not buying the individually wrapped items), now you'll also save the time of having to portion and bag them when making lunches or snacks each day during the week. This also produces less waste, so it's even environmentally friendly! Save individually packaged items for only when you really need to use them.

While you're shopping, if you come across an item that you use frequently and you find a great deal on it, grab extra! Stocking up on items you use regularly when they're at a cheaper price allows you to cut your grocery spending more in the long run. The longer you do this, the more you'll get to where you have a little of each of these items stocked up in your pantry, so you're able to wait until they're on sale again before needing to buy more (thus never having to pay the higher price for them). If you're worried about using all of something before it spoils (such as fresh produce), go home and split it into separate portions and freeze anything you aren't positive you'll use in the next couple of days. You can actually freeze a lot of foods that you might not think of; even dairy items (milk, cheese, sour cream, cream cheese, etc.) can be frozen, especially if they'll just be used to cook with (the texture on some may change slightly after being frozen, but it's only noticeable if you were to eat it straight by itself, rather than using it within a recipe). When you go to freeze something, also keep in mind how you usually use that item. If it's bell peppers that you generally cook with, slice or dice them up and freeze them that way. If it's heavy cream for your coffee, freeze it in ice cube trays and then dump the frozen cubes into a container or freezer bag – then you can easily grab just 1 or 2 for your coffee, or more if it's for a recipe!

If you're grocery shopping in person, look at the tops and bottoms of the shelves/aisles first– the most expensive (per ounce/serving) items are generally at eye level! The cheaper generic or store brand items are usually shelved high and low (especially low), so this is where your better prices will be; and there are very few things that are worth paying extra for a "name brand." Being brand loyal for a particular item is fine (there are certain ones that my family is very loyal to) – but for the *majority* of your groceries, no one is going to be able to tell a difference if you got the less expensive brand.

There are even additional ways you can save money on groceries that are specific to the type of item you're purchasing. For example, it is MUCH cheaper to buy bouillon cubes or powder, or bottles of concentrated stock, than to buy pre-made liquid chicken or beef broth. (Of course, it's even cheaper to make your own at home!) The packages of bouillon cubes/powder also often cost less if you get them from an ethnic food aisle, rather than the soup aisle at the store. Many meals that call for ground beef are just as good if made with ground turkey, which is cheaper (and less fattening)! Pounds of ground turkey or ground turkey sausage found in the freezer section are often even more economical. [*Extra hack*: you can give ground turkey a "beefier" flavor by adding some Worcestershire sauce, beef stock and/or Lawry's seasoning salt to the turkey as you brown it.]

Going back to the idea of trying to avoid having to throw out spoiled food (which obviously wastes money), has this ever happened to you? You go to make a recipe and it calls for milk, but then you realize that will use up most/all of the milk you have in your fridge, and you won't have enough for your kids' breakfasts in the morning (but you also really don't want to have to run to the store that night)?? Or you buy buttermilk for a specific recipe, only to have it go bad before you end up making the item (such as my grandmother's bran muffins)? No? Just me? Well, just in case you're worried this ever MIGHT happen to you, here's a tip for avoiding it: buy powdered milk!!! Yep, that simple. Powdered milk stays good for months/years and works just as well as refrigerated milk for cooking (drinking a glass of it is a different story and, in my opinion, would definitely have to be an acquired taste). There's even powdered buttermilk! Thank heavens for social media, since a post I made about my umpteenth "expired buttermilk means no bran muffins tonight" disaster resulted in a sweet friend clueing me in to the existence of powdered buttermilk. [Side note: elated about this newly discovered information, I called up my mom, who had had to listen to me both laugh and complain about the buttermilk conundrum numerous times over the years. Her response was a rather anticlimactic "Oh yep, they do." She KNEW!?!? She'd known for many years, and yet never thought to divulge that information to her darling daughter??? The level of betrayal is obviously astounding and still fresh.] [Another side note: Totally kidding about the betrayal. I love my mother and she's my best friend – but I did give her a hard time about not thinking to let me in on this little secret.]

Don't worry though, I got my grocery revenge on my mom once I discovered Amazon Fresh. If you live or work in an area that is eligible for Amazon Fresh grocery delivery, you should definitely be searching for sales and deals on there! It's only available in limited areas unfortunately (at least at the time I'm writing this), but if you're lucky enough to live or work where you have access to it [sorry Mom, hahaha!] it can be a HUGE money saver. Try searching for an item or category, and then sort your results by lowest cost – but still pay attention to the cost per ounce/unit and compare to your local grocery store prices if you're not positive that it's a great deal. When you find stellar prices on something, stock up! Sometimes these items are on sale because the warehouse is trying to move items off the shelves before they reach their "best by" date. Other times they simply have too many of them and need to make room, or perhaps the outer packaging was slightly damaged (in a way that doesn't impact the food), or maybe it's just a random flash sale. Simply score all the awesome grocery deals that you can, and then do your next round of meal planning based around some of these new items! I've done this before and been able to feed my family for pennies on the dollar, while still eating the types of meals that they're accustomed to. (For example, scoring some grocery items for literally coins meant my family got to have Mexican minestrone soup with ham and pasta for a grand total of $1.67 for the entire family!) Get creative and see which items you can combine (either with each other, or with items you already have in your pantry and freezer). Also don't forget that you can freeze items such as butter, vegetables, meat, and other items that you stock up on in order to keep them fresh longer. If you don't have Amazon Fresh delivery available in your area, do a little research to see if there are other options for you. Some stores (Kroger is one) have started opening grocery warehouses in areas where they don't have actual stores, and this allows them to offer grocery delivery to an area that they weren't otherwise serving. Be sure to see if the service you use has digital coupons or sales that can help you save additional money as well!

One of the best ways to learn how to save money on your groceries is to look at your own personal expenditures at the end of each month. Save all your grocery receipts for the month and then go back and look through them. See what items or categories accounted for the majority of what was spent from your grocery budget that month and then brainstorm ways that you might be able to save money on those items the next month. Seeing your own spending habits in black and white makes it easy (unfortunately sometimes) to see where you've been spending perhaps more money than necessary. Did you purchase lots of precooked meats? Then next month try to cook more meats ahead of time (and even freeze for use later in the month) or use more slow cooker recipes (if time was the issue). Are you spending lots on prepackaged snacks or precut produce? Remember as mentioned earlier how you can cut back on that. Were prepackaged sides (such as flavored rice and pastas) a "frequent flyer" in your grocery purchases? Look into how to make those yourself with the basic food item (such as rice) and seasonings to save money. If you've noticed a pattern in the last few sentences, it's that most food items that are a PRE-anything (precut, prepackaged, pre-seasoned, premade, etc.) means they cost you extra unnecessary money. They're convenience foods and while yes, they can be convenient, you are definitely paying for that luxury.

Another way to avoid having food go to waste is to not bring home food that your family won't actually eat! While it can be tempting to take advantage of a great "deal" on an item, it's not really a deal if you're not going to use it. It's especially unhelpful if you paid extra to get a "free" item. Ever been in the grocery store and seen a "deal of the week" or coupon where you get ABC for free if you buy XYZ? Sure, if you normally use both ABC and XYZ (including the specific brands involved in the "deal") then go for it! But what if you never use ABC? And what if you normally use a different brand or generic version of XYZ? Then HOW exactly is that a good deal for you?? Don't pay extra for "free" groceries. If the money you're spending is on an item you would truly use and get anyway, then you can always use the deal and then think creatively and proactively about using the extra "free" item. If you don't end up using it and it's still in your pantry when you do your next round of "use up stuff before the season changes or I buy more groceries," then go ahead and donate it to your locate food pantry or a friend so that it helps someone else before it goes bad. Free isn't actually a good deal if you end up throwing it out. I call this "realistic couponing." I don't use coupons to get things we wouldn't end up actually using, and I don't get something with a coupon if I can still get a different brand of it for less. I'm also not going to use up space filling some of my shelves with cleaning sprays or body wash that I don't actually need and would take forever to use up; but I WILL use space to stock up on things that I know will get used when I can get them for an amazing price.

Every so often (such as every few months, or when the weather season is about to change), set a goal to not purchase any groceries (other than things that you may go through weekly, such as milk) for a week or two. Use this time to intentionally eat through things that are in your freezer and pantry, so that nothing goes to waste. Take note of any upcoming expiration dates so that you can be sure to incorporate those items in your upcoming meals before they expire. Not only will this save you money, but it will also help prepare your pantry for the upcoming season to have more room for the types of foods that your family likes to eat during that time. If you find items that need to be used and you don't think your family is going to eat them, this is a great opportunity to donate them before they've expired.

A great money-saving tactic that combines meal-planning, grocery shopping and cooking all in one is what I like to call "ingredient stretching." First, choose meals for the week that have some ingredients in common. This will allow you to stretch these ingredients to cover more than one meal. If three of your meals for the week call for a 12 ounce can of XYZ (making 36 ounces total), then buy the large 30 ounce can at the store rather than three individual 12-ounce containers. (This is assuming that the 30-ounce can is cheaper than purchasing three 12-ounce cans, but that's a pretty safe bet.) Let's be clear – most dinner recipes (unlike baked goods such as cakes or cookies) don't require extreme preciseness on the amount/quantity of each ingredient. Using 10 ounces of diced tomatoes instead of 12 ounces isn't going to make or break the recipe for Aunt Helen's taco soup. Trust me. Using this method to both stretch/shrink the amount that you use in a recipe AND be able to buy the ingredient in a size/package that is more cost effective (of course after also using what you already have in your pantry) can have a HUGE impact on your monthly grocery budget. In fact, this is the main "hack" that allowed a friend and I to do freezer meal cooking together and make 30+ dinners for a family of four for only $100. We would brainstorm meal ideas, and then narrow it down so that the list mostly included meals that had multiple ingredients in common. We'd make a giant master grocery list by writing down the ingredients needed for each meal (using hash marks to note how many of the same item we needed, such as 15 12-ounce cans of diced tomatoes or 13 pounds of chicken). We even organized our shopping list according to the store setup in order to save time AND help avoid impulse purchases from wandering the aisles. Then we'd go grocery shopping and find the size and quantity that gave us the most "bang for our buck." Instead of buying fifteen 12-ounce cans (if you don't like math, that's 180 ounces), perhaps the most cost-effective option was to buy seven 24-ounce cans. Yes, that's only 168 ounces (again, if you don't like math – just trust me.) Once the "missing" 12 ounces were divided among 7 different recipes though, that means that each meal was missing less than 2 ounces from what its recipe called for. While playing fast and loose with ingredient quantities is not recommended if you're trying to make crème brûlée, I promise it won't even be noticed in your casserole. (Also, I have never in my life attempted to make crème brûlée, but I will definitely partake in eating it!)

Pay attention to the price per weight/unit for vegetables (or any ingredient) and compare the fresh, frozen, and canned options to find the best bang for your buck. While it is *usually* less expensive per ounce to buy a larger container of something, that's not the case every time. A few seconds to compare what you're really paying can add up to decent savings in the long run. If you're worried that some fresh veggies will start to wilt before you use them up in time, keep in mind that you can either chop and freeze them to use later or you can just put them in a meal that doesn't require them to be crisp anyway (such as a soup or stir fry).

Cooking…

So, you've come home from the grocery store (or thanked your pickup/delivery person) – now what?!? Before you start actually cooking, let's consider some ways you can save time and/or money right off the bat.

Make a list of quick, easy meals that your household enjoys and make sure you always have the ingredients for a few of them. Put these ingredients in their own basket/bin or somewhere that they're together and obviously separate from the rest of your groceries. (Do yourself another favor and label the bin!) This way, when one of those days comes (as they always do) when something unexpected happens, or you really don't want to cook what you had planned, or you (gasp) failed to plan for that day – boom! You already have everything you need for an easy, fast dinner that will be happily eaten! Want an even easier way to accomplish this tip? Keep one or two frozen pizzas in your freezer. Yes, I'm serious. If you're thinking "well duh, I already use pizza nights when I need an easy night," then let me ask you – do you use frozen pizzas, or do you do takeout/delivery? If it's the second one, then you may have the time-saving aspect down (although it's arguably often faster to use frozen oven pizza than to do takeout/delivery anyway) but you could still level-up on the money-saving part. Think frozen oven pizzas are gross? First, you may just need to branch out and try some new ones. If you're still not a fan though, why not keep some pizza dough/mix on hand to quickly make your own? This saves you money AND is healthier! You can even keep simple frozen cheese pizzas (or plain ready-to-cook pizza dough) on hand and just add on the toppings you feel like having that day before you pop it into the oven. [*Side note:* Did you know that they have pre-made ultra-thin pizza crusts at Dollar Tree? Spread on a little pizza/spaghetti/tomato sauce, sprinkle some cheese, add any toppings you already have, and bam – you have a pizza in the oven faster than your oven can preheat and for less than $3 total!]

If you're going to be cooking a meal that's easy to make (such as chili), then double (or even triple) it and make extra batches at the same time. Put the other in the freezer, and now you have an extra home-cooked meal on hand for another day, with very little effort. Ever heard the phrase "batch cooking?" That's what this is – and it's simple to do. Not only does this save you time down the road, but it can also save money since many meals can be "doubled" without actually having to spend double the price for ingredients. Remember the earlier tip about "ingredient stretching?" Continuing with chili as our example, let's say that the main ingredients for one batch of your chili are two pounds of ground beef, two 12-ounce cans of beans, and two 10-ounce cans of tomato juice. Instead of buying all these ingredients twice in order to make two batches of chili, try this instead: buy a 3-pound package of ground turkey (which is generally less per pound than ground beef) and split it. Yes, each batch will now have 1 ½ pounds instead of 2 pounds of meat, but that won't make a big difference when spread out amongst the whole pot. Buy a 48 ounce can of beans (provided it's cheaper per ounce than purchasing four 12-ounce cans) and split that between the two batches. Now, use a large 36-ounce bottle of tomato juice instead of four 10-ounce cans. Yes, I can do math – 36 ounces is not quite as much as 40 ounces. The trick is that having 2 ounces less in each batch (the "missing" 4 ounces spread over 2 batches) is negligible and won't be noticed while eating it. What WILL be noticed though, is that using this kind of scenario means that you can prepare two batches of chili for closer to only 1.5 times the cost of a single batch (rather than double the cost), if not less. The more often that you do this while cooking, the more the savings will add up! [*Side note:* When you do some batch cooking or even just double/triple a recipe you made, why not bring a freezer meal over to a neighbor or friend who has their own struggles going on in life right now? Everyone has them, everyone appreciates a home cooked meal that they didn't have to prepare, and putting happiness and good karma out into the world can only ever be a good thing.]

Another way to save money on groceries is to look up some depression-era recipes. These have started making a comeback recently, as more and more people have returned to thinking of food as a category where they can potentially ease the pinch on their bank account. Some recipes may take a little more time, but making your own bread, pasta, etc. can save significant money. (Side note: did you know that peanut butter bread was a thing?! Omg. Why did no one tell me about it sooner? My kids want to know why I'd been holding out on them.) Many depression-era recipes also use only shelf-stable ingredients, so you can often make these items without needing a trip to the grocery store since you could already have everything on hand (which saves you time AND money)!

Even if you don't mind cooking, chances are you don't want to spend all day in the kitchen. There are plenty of ways to spend less time cooking meals though. First, let's start with the obvious (and no, I don't mean calling for take-out) – slow cookers and InstantPots are a busy mom's best friends! Any recipe that only requires me to dump everything into my slow cooker in the morning and turn it on is a winner in my book. If that didn't happen in the morning though, my InstantPot is waiting when I get home to save the day! (Beef stew in 20 minutes anyone?) Use an Instant Pot to brown multiple pounds of ground meat at a time, or to cook multiple pounds/breasts of chicken. It's a great time saver since you don't have to stand there actively cooking, plus it's an easy way to prep a large amount of meat that you can then freeze to use in meals later on!

Let's also not forget the snazzy newcomer on the kitchen appliance scene – the air fryer. (Personally, I'm a fan of the toaster oven style air fryers, as opposed to basket style ones, simply because they widen your cooking options even more.) Not only can it cook foods in a fraction of the time that a conventional oven takes, it also doesn't heat up your kitchen or use as much electricity (some extra hidden savings). Between those three small appliances, I've gone months before without ever using my actual oven! Banana bread in the slow cooker…homemade personal pizzas in the air fryer oven…chicken piccata in the InstantPot…berry cobbler in the air fryer…. The list goes on and on. Look at the small appliances that you already have on hand and start yourself some new boards on Pinterest (grouped by appliance/method of cooking) – the possibilities are endless!

While I'm definitely a huge fan of useful small kitchen appliances, saving time and money in the kitchen can still be done without them. Let's turn to the old faithful freezer for instance. Many foods can be made ahead of time and frozen. This saves you time AND money! I'm not just talking about "freezer meals" (though we'll get to those too). There are actually very few foods that *can't* be frozen! Breakfast items, crowd-pleasing snacks, quick re-heat lunch/dinner items, casseroles, entire entrees, and dinners…the list is practically endless. Having a hard time thinking of what you could make to freeze (especially if you're trying to use ingredients you already have)? Start by thinking about the "convenience" foods you're buying that you could make for less yourself. For breakfast, try making batches of pancakes, French toast, or muffins and freeze them! Just pull out muffins the night before to thaw or pop some pancakes or French toast into the toaster (or microwave) in the morning and you're good to go. It's quick AND saves you money to make and freeze them yourself instead of buying a box of pre-made ones at the store. [Quick tip: If the pancakes come out of the toaster a little too dry, drizzle a little syrup on them and then pop in the microwave for 30 seconds – perfect!]

Ready for an extra time-saving hack for pancakes? You can make them in your oven! Yep, you read that right – pancakes that don't require you to stand at the stove pouring and flipping one or two at a time. Simply make a bowl of pancake batter, spray a sheet pan (or two) with nonstick spray, and pour the batter into the pan. They will rise some as they cook, of course, so don't fill the pan too high. Then bake in your oven (I cook mine for 20 minutes at 385°F, but you may need to adjust that for your particular oven). Once they're done, cut into rectangles and you have pancakes ready to eat or freeze for later! They come out thick and fluffy this way, and honestly it's now my kids' preferred pancake method. Plus, you can do several pans at a time and be handling other tasks while they bake – thus saving you plenty of cooking time AND giving you a nice sized batch of prepped breakfast items to keep on hand!

Every meal or snack time has items that you can prepare in advance and have waiting in your freezer. Have kids that love those crustless sealed peanut butter and jelly sandwiches? Yep – you can make those yourself and keep them in the freezer. My kids also love our homemade breakfast "egg-wiches" and sausage and egg English muffins (and you guessed it – I make batches every so often and store them in the freezer). Another of their favorites is our homemade granola bars – they can be made quickly, they don't require cooking, and you can either keep them all in a container on your counter (if your family will eat them all that week), or you can freeze some and thaw them later to enjoy. If you're still having a hard time thinking of items to make and freeze (or you're just wanting to add in more variety), then go check out the freezer aisles the next time you're at the grocery store and look at the sections with pre-made foods. Chances are good that if the store sells it in the freezer section, then it's something you can make yourself at home (for less money) and freeze yourself!

A great pantry item to keep on hand (especially if you have children) is inexpensive flavored muffin mix (such as the Martha White brand – lots of flavors and they're around $1 per package). Not only can you use these to make muffins (of any size), but you can even use them to make flavored pancakes or waffles (and of course you could freeze some of those too)! While not as cost-effective as making your own plain pancakes from scratch, they're easy to whip up quickly and can serve as something a little different or a treat in place of going out for breakfast on the weekend (thus saving money). Mini muffins are easy to freeze and be able to pull out just a few in the morning to add into a kid's school lunchbox too!

Another tip is to cook more than you eat and eat more often than you cook. I'm not suggesting that you try to eat a larger amount of food than you currently do (we're not going for gluttony here), but rather that you get smart about your cooking so that you can eat more *often* than you actually had to work in the kitchen. What does that mean? It's simple, and it's one of the oldest time-tested ways of being frugal in the kitchen – in a word, leftovers. (Yep, I said it.) Cooking more than you/your family will eat at that meal will, obviously, result in leftovers. Having leftovers means you can eat more often than you actually cook (which saves you time, WITHOUT requiring that you eat out or grab fast foo take-out). If your initial response is something like "but I hate leftovers" or "my husband/kids won't eat them," hear me out. Making use of leftovers doesn't necessarily mean you have to eat the exact same thing the next day. It CAN mean that (and in my house it often does), but it doesn't have to. Be creative with revamping leftovers if you don't like to eat the exact same meal several times in a row. Made soup last night? Thicken it up and serve it over rice tonight. Had roast with mashed potatoes and green beans yesterday? Use the leftover meat to make roast beef sandwiches today. Maybe you had a roasted rotisserie chicken and some vegetables on Monday…then why not use the leftover chicken to make a quick chicken tortilla soup on Tuesday, and then some chicken salad on Wednesday? Like so many things we're discussing in this book, this tip is all about thinking ahead creatively so you can be more efficient with your time and your finances. Depending on the meal or method of cooking, embracing this can even help save money on your utility bills because you won't be using your oven every night. Cook smarter, not harder (or more often)!

Using leftovers in combination with your freezer can open up all sorts of possibilities that you may not have considered yet. For instance, have you ever had leftovers of a soup or stew (but not enough left to feed the family for another night, even if you stretched it or added to it), that you just tossed out? Instead of wasting what might seem like "not enough," try freezing it in plastic disposable party cups. Simply pop it out of the cup once frozen (tear the cup away if necessary) and put it into a freezer bag to store. This way it's in individual serving sizes, and it's easy to either toss several into a pot to heat up on the stove or put one into a large glass microwave-safe dish (such as a thick glass measuring cup, since the frozen cup shape will fit) to warm in the microwave. Having pre-made individual portions like this can come in handy if you have *almost* enough leftovers of something else one night and want to have small portions of soup with it, or just let one or two people have soup while the rest finish the other leftovers. They're also great to grab when someone's sick, or when a family member is home alone for dinner one night.

Although this "progressive leftovers" tip can be used spontaneously when you end up with leftovers you didn't expect, it can also be thought out in advance as part of your meal planning. For example, here's an easy dinner progression idea: put some raw chicken breasts and some salsa verde in the slow cooker (or put them in a freezer bag and freeze for later, then when it's "later" take them out and throw them in). Cook (3-4 hours on high or 7-8 hours on low) and then shred the chicken. Now you can use it for several dinners! On the first night, put the chicken mixture in tortillas or taco shells with some rice, avocado, and shredded cheese for chicken verde tacos/burritos. You can also put some with shredded cheese in between tortillas and make quesadillas. The next night, mix in a little cream of chicken soup with some of the chicken verde mixture and serve it over rice. On the third night, take what's left, add in some cream of chicken soup, chicken broth, white beans, and chili seasonings and whip up some white chicken chili! Or, add chicken broth, corn, black beans, shredded cheese, and tomatoes and have chicken taco soup that you can garnish with avocado. Got a bit of chicken taco soup still leftover? Drain the liquid out and put the rest over chips as chicken verde nachos. The possibilities are endless! Thinking creatively can have such an impact on your budget and the time you have to spend making meals.

Speaking of leftovers… If you're having leftovers one night and don't have something else that you need to be doing during the time you'd otherwise be cooking (you know, if there weren't leftovers), then consider using that time to get ahead food-wise. Cook up some breakfast foods to freeze for the coming weeks (muffins, egg muffins, pancakes, waffles, scrambled eggs and sausage for toaster sandwiches or breakfast tacos, etc.). If you don't need breakfast items, try browning some ground meat or cooking and shredding some chicken, and then bag the meats to freeze for later use (which saves you time on that step when making dinner sometime in the future).

Saving even more time…

Training yourself to think ahead for ways that you can help "Future You" (more on her later) can make exponentially more difference in your schedule and stress level than you may think. Here's just a few examples of ways you can save yourself time and effort in the future by using a few extra minutes wisely right now:

On Sunday (or whatever meal prep day you choose), cut up any fresh veggies and fruit that will be needed for the week. Now that's one less thing you have to do to get dinner or snacks ready for the other days! If you choose to expand this into what many people think of as full-on "meal prepping," great! Even if you don't though, just this one small preparation will make you appreciate the effort all week long.

For recipes that you make fairly often that require seasonings that aren't in a pre-made packet, consider making your own pre-made seasoning packets for them! For example, if your family loves your homemade taco soup and you use 5 different spices/seasonings when you make it, then instead of having to measure those out separately every time you want to throw together taco soup try making several helpings of the spices ahead of time. Use tiny food or condiment containers (or plastic sandwich baggies) and put a removable label on each with "taco soup" and today's date on it (or write on the baggie with a permanent marker). Now the next few times that you want to make the soup, you won't have to spend time pulling out the recipe to remind yourself how much of each spice to use, gathering your measuring spoons, opening and measuring out each seasoning, etc. This can also be extra helpful if someone is going to pitch in and help make dinner one night – you can tell them to just grab one of the labeled containers and add the other ingredients, without them having to find your recipe or measure out items either! If you're lacking space in your kitchen or pantry, you can also do this but not separate them out into individual containers; simply make one bag or container that says "taco soup seasonings," and list how much to use for 1 recipe. (Just be sure to shake and mix it up first before scooping out a recipe's portion, if you do it that way.) Like many time-saving tips, this requires just a small time investment on the front end – but pays off numerous times in the future.

Along a similar vein, another idea is to set aside time one day a month (or however often you choose) to pre-cook certain ingredients (particularly meat) that you use in many of your common meals, such as taco meat, cooked shredded chicken, etc. This allows you to have meat handy and already prepared, so that you can pull it out the night before (or even the same afternoon if necessary) to thaw and save yourself the most time-consuming part of making those meals. They also come in handy if there's a sudden change in schedule or something else that makes preparing the dinner you had intended that evening no longer a practical option and allows you to pivot to a new home-cooked meal for the night rather than having to resort to take-out or fast food.

If you're home during the day and will be cooking dinner that evening, why not use a few 5-minute pockets of time to do some of your dinner prep (cutting up veggies, etc.) in advance? When dinnertime rolls around, you'll have much less to do, and cooking will be a breeze! That could even lead to [gasp] having a little spare time that night for some self-care, tackling another small item on your to-do list, or SLEEP!

As you can see by now, the overriding theme for these tips is to work and cook smarter, not harder (or more). If you're one of the many (or most) women who feel tired, frazzled, and short on time in the evenings, then anything you can do now to save yourself some time (and sanity) later is exponentially worth it. Even for tasks that will take the same amount of *actual* time to complete no matter when you do them, having the luxury of not having to do that task (because you prepped it beforehand) at the end of a particularly tiresome day can make all the difference.

Random Little Bits…

In many chapters (starting with this one), you'll find a section at the end with a random assortment of miscellaneous "tidbits" – ideas that don't need a whole paragraph, but they may be the solution to an annoying little problem that you didn't even know you had!

- Store sliced carrots and celery in jars of water in the refrigerator. Storing them submerged in water (as opposed to in a dry container) will help them last WEEKS longer before wilting! This works on other fresh produce too.
- Put a small bin or basket on a prominent (eye level) shelf in your fridge and label it "EAT FIRST" – then use it to house any fresh produce or leftovers that are in danger of spoiling.
- Cook bacon in the oven on a foil or parchment paper lined baking sheet for easy cleanup. Even better – cook it in an air fryer oven (I'll never cook bake another way again)!
- Want to make grocery shopping more fun while also saving time and money? Try setting a timer on your phone and play your own personal version of Supermarket Sweep! Get in, get out.
- When browning ground meat, use aluminum foil to make a "bowl" to pour the fat and grease into. Once it cools, simply

fold up the foil and toss it in the garbage. Now you haven't committed the horrible plumbing sin of pouring it down the kitchen sink drain, and you also don't have to worry about it finding a hole in your garbage bag to leak through.

Chapter 2: Feeding the Masses (Meal-planning)

Did reading the words "meal planning" just make you cringe? If you're picturing rows of containers all full of the exact same portions of bland chicken, brown rice and chopped veggies and it's making you start to get hives, relax – that's not the kind of meal-planning I'm talking about. You may be picturing that because of seeing people post photos on social media of doing their "meal prep" for the week, often if they have nutritional macros that they're trying to maintain. That's great (for them), but it's not for everyone. If you ARE someone who does this or is interested in trying that, by all means – go for it! What we're going to look at though are ways that planning and prepping can be used to save you time and money (without having to eat the same thing every day, or even if you do).

This is definitely a topic where the "spaghetti method" comes into play. You can't try to implement all of the suggestions we're going to go over here. You literally can't – some of them completely contradict each other! This is a great example of why this book helps anyone and everyone, because there are a range of tips and ideas from different viewpoints. Does your family find comfort in having their favorite meals often? There are tips in here to help you plan that. Are they the exact opposite and think variety is the spice of life (pun intended) when it comes to their meals? There are suggestions for meal planning with that in mind too! Chances are that as you read through these ideas, the ones that resonate with you and your family's own lifestyle will jump out at you – choose those to start with, and then tweak things from there. No matter which suggestions appeal to you, they all have the same goal of helping you find simple methods to save time and money so that you have more to devote to the more fun and fulfilling parts of your life.

Planning…

Let's look at the actual planning part first (then we'll add in some ways to help your groceries and meals stretch farther). Like I said, this is definitely a "spaghetti theory" portion of the book because there are numerous different ways to approach it. See what appeals to you or sounds like it would be the most helpful for your daily life and go from there!

So, what exactly IS meal planning? It's as simple as planning for what meals (or types of meals) you're going to fix for the upcoming days. (Often, I may discuss this only in terms of dinners, since that's typically the largest meal that most families eat, and the one that can get most expensive and require the most time, but meal planning can be used for any and every meal or snack that your household consumes.) Exactly how and how long in advance (and for which daily meals) you decide to plan is completely up to you! Some people like to plan out an entire month at a time, with each day's meals already predetermined and written on a calendar. Some people feel claustrophobic at the mere thought of being "locked in" to what they'll have for dinner for an entire month, so they only plan ahead a week or a few days at a time (or not at all, but we're about to discuss why that's not helpful). Others, like myself, fall somewhere in between and try to plan meals for 1-2 weeks at a time, while still maintaining some flexibility on what dinners will be made on which nights. Again, you figure out what works for you – regardless of what meal planning ends up looking like for you, the upcoming tips and tricks will help ensure that it serves to save you time and money!

You'll notice that many of these tips also correspond well with some of the ideas shared in the cooking section, since meal planning, meal prepping, and cooking all go hand in hand and can work together to help your groceries (and the hard-earned money you paid for them) stretch farther. So, on to some suggestions and tips for how to make meal planning and prepping work for you...

Meal Planning 101:

Let's just address this now: the first time you do this (if you don't already meal plan), it may take awhile. Like trying out any new skill (which is what this is), you'll be slower and more unsure of yourself at first. Does that mean you should stop, or say "well obviously this isn't for me"? No!! Trying new routines takes more time at first, no matter what it is. This does NOT mean that you're not good at it, or that it won't help you, or that it will always take this long, or that it's not worth your time, or that you can't make this part of your regular routine going forward. It simply means that it's new. Think of a simple family favorite recipe (we'll use spaghetti, but just think of a simple meal that your family loves) – does it take genuine, conscious effort and focused thought to make? Nope, because you've made it so many times. The same will happen with meal planning and just about any other tip or suggestion in this book. Give yourself grace and acknowledge that there may be some "growing pains" or a small learning curve, but you are MORE than capable of making these simple, but profoundly rewarding changes for you and your family. Future You deserves it – be kind and do this for her.

When meal planning, consider having "themed" nights of the week. Most people take this to mean that "theme" covers the type of food (Mediterranean Monday, Taco Tuesday, Soup Sunday, etc.). Depending on your schedule though, perhaps the "theme" needs to be centered around HOW the food is cooked. Right now, my kids are in a season where we have lessons and practices on certain nights of the week, so the method of cooking is what I focus on (at least for those nights). I know that Mondays and Wednesdays are packed right up until dinnertime, so I plan on those being slow cooker dinners – this way I can set it up in the morning and know that when we walk back in the door that evening that dinner is already done. Thursdays and Fridays are when our activities are later in the evening, so I have a break during which I can cook – but it needs to be something that can be eaten more quickly. Sundays are generally our calmest day – so if I feel like trying out a new recipe or cooking something that's more time-intensive, then this is the day that I plan for that. Regardless of which version of "themed nights" works best for you and your household, planning in this way can help simplify meal planning for you so that you're less stressed about deciding what to eat on those days and getting it ready.

When you're looking at the calendar for your upcoming week to plan meals, also think about what you have scheduled that week that may be out of the ordinary. Do you have an extra appointment on Tuesday, or you have to go sit at your son's baseball practice on Wednesday? Are these times that you might get hungry (or just munchy) and want a snack? Then save yourself a little money by planning ahead and bringing a snack with you in the car so that you're not tempted to go through a drive-thru while you're out or over-eat when you get home because you're too hungry. Meal planning isn't *only* about choosing meals for eating at home.

If you like to look at recipes on Pinterest, make a board for "recipes to try." Once you try one, spend the extra 3 seconds RIGHT THEN to either print it out to keep (if that's something you can do quickly), or save it to a "tried and liked" board (and delete it from the "to try" board since you've tried it now, so that one doesn't get clogged up), or delete it from your Pinterest account entirely if you didn't like it. Now the recipe is dealt with, and you won't have to wonder months from now whether that's the one you tried before or not and whether you liked it or not! You can also do this same process with items that you take a screenshot of with your phone (you can even set up folders like this in your camera album to organize them) and ones that you save on Facebook.

You can choose whatever days(s) works for you, but in our house, weekends are when we focus on food. This means first looking through the food/groceries we have on hand, both to see what we already have to work with AND to see what needs to be used up before it goes bad. Once I know what we already have that we need to use, then I can turn to meal planning or making any necessary changes in what I might have already planned for the upcoming week (since being flexible in your own plans can be key to saving money on food). If you need to get groceries, this is a great time to place an online pickup/delivery order right then while you're planning and everything is fresh on your mind! This also allows you to either order groceries or make your own shopping list while you're already thinking on your planned meals AND you're at home to be able to check your pantry for anything else you think of and wonder whether you have enough. Weekends are also when I prep breakfasts & lunches for the week (including replenishing my freezer stock of pre-made pancakes, crustless sandwiches, etc. if needed) and prep dinners for Monday and Tuesday if possible.

To help avoid any dinnertime drama, make sure your family knows what's coming meal-wise for the week. If cooking and meal prep duties are shared between several members of your household, make it easier on everyone and try to sit down to meal plan together. Use a different color pen for each person (so it's easy at a glance to see who's cooking that night on the calendar). Have somewhere in your kitchen to display the upcoming week's meals (or the whole month if you want). Not only does this help keep everyone on the same page as far as who's cooking and what's going to be for dinner, but it can even help with picky kids who may see that a meal they don't care for is coming up since they can also see that a favorite will be coming right after that!

I recommend writing your meal plan (regardless of how many days/weeks it covers) on/with something that can be erased (pencil and paper, dry erase board, etc.). Personally, I plan several weeks at a time with pencil on a paper calendar, but then I also have a laminated "chalkboard" (it's a black paper with white writing so it looks like a chalkboard) that shows one week at a time and can be written on with liquid chalk marker (you could also laminate a white paper and use dry erase markers on it). The paper version stays with me in my life-spiral (more on that later), and the laminated "chalkboard" stays on the side of our refrigerator. Having them all be erasable makes it easy to make changes as necessary if your schedule or plans change, or you end up having unexpected leftovers one night, etc.

Next Level Momma...

This particular suggestion takes meal planning to a whole new level. While it may take a bit more time and effort initially than many of the other ideas, I promise it is SO worth it. First, consider how many nights a week you usually cook (we'll say 5; maybe the others are leftovers and pizza night). Next, consider how many weeks you'd like to do this for (keep reading to see what I mean) – for this example we'll say 12. 12 weeks is roughly 3 months, and with 5 dinners per week that makes 60 dinners. Now, make a separate list or page for each week and number them, and then grab your recipe binder. For each week, write down 5 dinners (you do NOT have to use 60 different ones, you can repeat family favorites – just try to space them out so there are several weeks in between). Under the name of each meal, write down its list of ingredients (you can just write the ingredient itself, not the specific measurement). If your current schedule or routine is such that you know you function best with having 3 crockpot or "toss & go" meals planned for the week (as we've discussed earlier), then keep this in mind while making your lists and choose your meals for each week accordingly. When I first did this, I made sure to have at least 3 easy meals (such as crockpot ones or toss-and-go soups) on each week, and I wrote next to each meal whether it required the crockpot, InstantPot, stovetop, etc. Once you've done this, you now have 3 MONTHS worth of dinner meal-planning done!!! Seriously, you just took care of several steps that you'd otherwise have to do repeatedly every single week. Now THAT'S a great way to be kind to "Future You!" This one may not be a super *quick* tip (though you can get it done in an evening or two) – but it's one that will reward you for YEARS to come.

If your family's preferred dinners tend to fluctuate with the time of year (such as you like to grill outside a lot during the summer or prefer to have lots of soups and stews during winter months), then keep this in mind as well when making your lists. If it's spring now, sit down and make 12 weeks' worth of summer dinner lists (or whatever next season is about to come) and you'll have those ready to start rotating through soon! If you do this just once every few months, you'll quickly have an entire YEAR'S worth of dinner menus saved up, with a different set for each season. Want to really take this to the next level and really have Future You wanting to kiss Current You every single week? Once you have your lists made, then hop onto the app or website for whichever store you typically place your grocery pickup/delivery orders with and see if it will allow you to make saved lists. Be sure to check both their app and their website, as some stores (such as Walmart, at the time this was written) can only handle lists on their website but others (such as H-E-B) will allow it through the app as well. Take one week's list of dinners at a time and make a grocery list for those meals; include all the items on your list, even if right now you have plenty of that item in stock. Save the lists separately, titled by week ("Dinners Week 2", "Dinners Week 7", etc.). Now before you go to place your grocery order for that week (or two weeks, however you do it), you only have to decide which weeks' lists you're using (the easiest way is to go in order and just cycle through them all before starting again) and tell it to add those items to your cart. You can remove any items you know you still have plenty in stock of at home, and then you're done!

Another suggestion if you do this is to then clip the recipes for each week behind that week's list in your recipe binder (more tips on a recipe binder coming up). This way you won't have to flip through searching for the recipes for that week, and if you're ever randomly wanting to find a certain one then it's easy to just look at the lists on the front of each group and find which week it's in. The remainder of the recipes in your recipe binder can still be left in their usual categories, so that if you want to sub in one of those or make it to freeze then you can easily find it in its section of the binder. If you don't want to keep the recipes with their corresponding week, then when you meal plan for the upcoming week just pull out the recipes you're going to be using so that they're handy (especially if anyone else may be pitching in to help cook). You can put a post-it note or sticky tab in your recipe binder to mark the spot that you took them from if you want to be sure they go back into the same place/order in the binder when that meal has been made.

Not a "paper person"? No problem! You can still do this same concept, just use Pinterest. Make a board for each week (titled Week 1, etc.) and save the recipes for that week on each individual board. You can even upload your own recipes (or photos of them) onto the board if they're not ones you got from Pinterest! Or, keep the lists in the notes app on your phone; if you have photos of the recipes, you can even attach them to each note! You can also simply take pics of the recipes and then save them in separate labeled albums ("Dinners Week 1", etc.) in the camera roll on your phone. There are numerous phone apps as well that are great for helping to organize your meal planning, which can also be helpful if you want to be able to share it with a partner's phone or view it on different devices.

The Planning is in the Details...

Most people have a grocery list on the side of their refrigerator or somewhere in their kitchen that they use to write down items needed at the store. Try adding a second list too though – items in your kitchen/pantry that need to be used up! Random items that have been in the freezer for awhile or are in your pantry and getting close to expiration date. Then the next time you meal plan, you can look at the "to use" list and try to incorporate some of these into your next few meals!

Another great time saver is to make out a grocery pickup order AS you're planning out your meals. Once you have your meals chosen and see what ingredients you need that you don't already have on hand, add them to a grocery order while you're looking at your meals. Schedule a pickup or delivery for the day (or day before) you plan to do any prep cooking. You can also keep a running grocery order going to add miscellaneous items to during the week as you run out of them; then you'll simply be adding your meal planning ingredients to the order and scheduling it! Not only does this save you time, but it can also save you money since it keeps you from walking through the aisles yourself and grabbing impulse purchases or items that you can't remember whether you still have enough on hand or not (something you can easily check for if you're placing the order while at home)!

If you want to let your family have input on dinners you're planning, designate one night that your spouse gets to pick, one night for each kid, etc. They still have to choose in advance so that you can incorporate it into your plan and shopping for the week, but it helps cut down on complaints that someone doesn't like any of the dinners that week! If you're worried that little Sarah will pick spaghetti every single week because it's her favorite (and the rest of the family will get sick of it), try having each member of the household think of their 6 favorite meals and write them on slips of paper. Then you can pick one of these from a jar (or wherever you keep them) for that person's "night of choice" that week, ensuring that Sarah's favorite spaghetti will only get repeated once every 6 weeks or so!

Do you enjoy trying new recipes, but also need the benefits that meal planning and prepping provide? Try designating one night each week as "new recipe night". You can use tried and true meals for the weekdays when you're more pressed for time, and yet still be able to test out a new dinner on Sunday (or whatever night you choose) when you have a bit more time to devote to cooking (since sometimes trying a new recipe inherently takes longer than one you've made hundreds of times).

When you meal plan for the week, another idea is to have a few small bins/baskets to use in your pantry and put the items that go with each meal in a basket (one basket/bin for each dinner that week). Obviously, things that are refrigerated or frozen won't be able to go in there (unless you want to put a basket in the fridge if a meal is all refrigerated ingredients), but simply having the items for that meal already gathered together can make cooking that evening feel simpler and lessen your mental load.

Planning your meals and doing online grocery shopping (if possible) will save you money! It lets you be intentional with what you're buying, so you're not wasting money on items you don't have a real purpose for or that are impulse purchases. It's been researched and proven that the less often you're in a grocery store, the less money you'll spend. (This is one added benefit for those that feel comfortable meal planning an entire month in advance.) For items that have to be purchased throughout the month (milk, fresh produce, etc.), be strict with yourself and only get those items (no impulse buys) when you shop. Planning this way saves you time as well because you can arrive at the store with a list and plan in hand – no need to wander aimlessly down the aisles trying to decide what "sounds good" to cook that week!

If you're really trying to cut down spending on your grocery budget, look at your local stores' sale ads before doing your meal planning. If you can get a great deal on chicken this week, then plan lots of chicken meals! See what sale items you can combine to make multiple meals (don't forget to look at what you already have on hand at home as well). For example, if you can get a great deal on chicken, potatoes, and broccoli, then plan on having roasted chicken, baked potatoes and steamed broccoli one night; then dice up some carrots you already had and add some rice to make a chicken stir fry the next night; last, toss everything that's left (and any other veggies you might have) into a pot with some chicken broth and make a homemade chicken soup for another dinner! Another great tip for when you find a good price on meat (chicken, ground meat, pork chops, etc.) is to either cook it now and freeze it in meal-size portions, or divide it up into meal-size portions before you freeze it (this is especially helpful for situations like finding a great deal on a "family pack" with 12 pork chops, if your household would normally only eat 4 in one night; this way you don't have to eat pork chops for 3 meals in a row, and you also don't have to worry about any going bad or going to waste).

Stretching…

One of the less-thought-about ways that meal planning can save you time AND money is that it allows you to be intentional about stretching your food and groceries farther. With little effort, you can make a small amount of leftovers from one night turn into a completely different meal for the next night – rather than having the leftovers get shoved to the back of the fridge and only thrown out when they're on the verge of being able to walk themselves out. Having leftovers from a meal doesn't mean you have to eat the exact same thing the next night in order to not waste the food!

One way is to use leftovers in a different way so that they feel like a "new" meal. For instance, let's say that you made Green Chile Chicken Enchilada Soup one night and have leftovers – simply put it over rice the next night to stretch it farther. Or maybe you make a taco bake casserole on Tuesday, and then put the leftovers inside tortillas and grill them for quick quesadillas on Wednesday! If you made chili for dinner one night, try using some of what's left to make "chili lasagna" another night, and "personal taco bags" (a small bag of tortilla chips or Fritos, with chili or taco meat, lettuce, tomato, sour cream, cheese, etc.) for another. Made a large pot of tortilla soup and still have some left? Strain out the liquid and put what's left over tortilla chips for loaded out nachos. Still have a bit more left? Use it as the stuffing for a southwestern omelet. Here's a "pro tip" for you – almost any leftover meat and/or vegetables can be turned into an omelet, loaded scrambled eggs, ingredients in a stir fry, or toppings for homemade pizza! I've purposefully talked this through out loud around my kids while I was meal planning, so now they involve themselves in it sometimes too! "Ooh Mom, we're having barbecue chicken next week? Can we make sure there's some left and make Hawaiian barbecue chicken quesadillas for the next dinner?"

If you have a large amount of leftovers one night and haven't included them already in your planned meals for the week, then either sub the leftovers in for another night that week (one less night to cook!) or package and freeze them (be sure to label and date) to be able to use later! Most weeks I plan on having leftovers for 1 or 2 nights that week, but if I end up with more leftovers than anticipated I generally freeze them (unless it's something that doesn't freeze well, like cooked pasta – those leftovers have to get used that same week). I do this even if it's only a serving or two. Then once a month or so, we'll have a "frozen leftovers night" where I pull out enough leftovers from the freezer the night before to feed everyone. If there were several meals that had small portions left (not enough to feed the whole family), then I pull out several of those and everyone gets to have a choice in which they eat for dinner. The kids love those nights too because it often means that each of them gets to have their favorite meal for dinner since they don't have to be eating the same thing. Doing this saves money AND time – a busy mom's most precious commodities!

Whichever day of the week is generally your meal-planning/cooking day, get into the habit of having "fridge cleanout" meals the day before. This helps ensure that leftovers get used (so you're not wasting food and money), saves you the time of having to cook additional meals that day, AND it helps clean your fridge and freezer out to have ample space available to store new groceries and meals for the coming week.

Once a month or so, do a round of "pantry cooking"! (You'll need to do this less often if you "pantry shop" each week while meal planning.) A "pantry cooking" week means that you try not to purchase ANY groceries that week and you only make meals with items you already have on hand. This has multiple benefits. It helps keep you from having to throw out expired food that you just "never got around to" cooking. It also can force you to use any random items that you have that you don't normally buy (perhaps ones that came free with another grocery purchase or that were random impulse buys). Pantry cooking can also help you see whether there's certain items that you've been over-buying lately, or ones that perhaps your family used to enjoy eating but now tastes have changed, and no one has gravitated toward those foods in quite some time.

Recipe binder tips:

Before we leave the cooking subject, let's wrap up with a few ideas you might want to try for keeping track of your recipes. First, I highly suggest a 3-ring binder for keeping them, rather than a recipe card box. Chances are that most of your recipes are printed out anyway (or they're saved somewhere so that you *could* print them out), so the ease and versatility of a binder just makes more sense than having to be limited to cards in a box.

Having a recipe binder makes it easy to add in pages you print from online/Pinterest/email/Facebook/whatever or tear out of a magazine; use page protectors for ones you can't or don't want to hole punch, and page protectors or card-holder pages (easily available online or at Walmart or an office supply store) for recipe cards that you already have.

Having your recipes in a binder also means you can divide/group them into as many categories or sections as you want. Categorize by what makes sense to YOU and how/what you tend to cook. Sure, the traditional way is to have categories for meats, main dishes, sides, etc. What if what works best for you is to group items a different way though? While my recipe binder does have sections for side dishes, desserts, breads, and breakfast, I have my meat/main dish/casserole/full meal recipes grouped by *how I cook them*! There are separate sections for oven/stovetop meals, slow cooker, InstantPot and air fryer recipes. (For dishes that can be cooked in more than one way, I put them in the section for how I usually tend to cook it; you could also print multiple copies to have in each section though.) Is that how I was "taught" to keep them? Nope. But you better believe that it makes a huge difference in how quickly I can meal plan since I can easily flip to sections of recipes that are what I need to fit into our schedule on certain days.

Treat your recipe binder like your closet – don't waste space by keeping stuff in there that you don't use! If you try a recipe and no one cares for it, take it out of the binder. Got some family favorites or ones that you gravitate to when life is rough and you don't truly feel like cooking? Keep those near the front of their section. Have some that you want to keep but you only make them once or twice a year? Keep them at the back of their sections (or make a section just for holiday/specialty items) so you don't have to keep flipping past them every time you plan meals. If there are certain recipes that are your go-to meals if you want to batch cook or make a meal to give someone else, try using little colored sticky tabs (or cut a post-it note into strips) to mark those in your binder for quick reference. Keep your recipe binder organized in a way that makes sense for how and what you like to cook!

Chapter 3: The Dreaded Tasks – Cleaning and Laundry

We've been rockin' right along with ways to save time and money while feeding your family. You're excited and feeling the high of inspiration, right?! Then you turned the page and read the dreaded words – cleaning and laundry. Boo, hiss. [*insert shudders here*] Stick with me though!

This is not a guide on "how you too can keep your baseboards and blinds spotless 24/7 and happily scrub behind your toilets every day." If that's what you're looking for, you picked the wrong book, friend. Remember that I mentioned in the introduction that I'm proof that things and people can change? Yeah…let's just say that I had to learn a lot of these things the hard way, including how to keep the state of our house at a manageable level. Ever shoved a few dirty dishes in the oven in a panic to hide them from guests because you didn't have time to finish cleaning? Yep, you're not alone. If you *also* then forgot that and turned the oven on to preheat later that evening and accidentally melted what was hiding in there…welcome to the club, my friend. (If not, no judging!) So, when I say that I've been there, *I've been there!* And I can tell you that there's hope – there are simple, time-saving ways to reform the bad habits that may have led us to that point. We're going to focus on small changes and some different "hacks" that will help save you time and frustration and make it easier for these chores to get accomplished efficiently – so that everyone in the household can enjoy your home and each other more.

If discussing "cleaning the house" involves you thinking about picking up piles of paper and laundry, gathering up stuff to "put it away" or things like this – then prepare yourself. That's actually NOT cleaning! That's tidying up (or "picking up"), and that has to do with how much stuff and clutter is in your house, as well as the routines you have (or don't have) in place to handle them. Cleaning means sanitizing and wiping down surfaces – not getting them *ready* to be wiped off. In truth, these do go hand in hand though. An uncluttered house LOOKS cleaner, regardless of whether it truly is or not. It's just simply a fact. Friends often come to our home and comment about it being "so clean" – HA! The joke's on them. I do keep counters and the dining table wiped off and try to make sure the bathrooms never get too "scary," but my home is rarely (okay, never) spotless. What it IS is uncluttered – and that's what helps it give the impression that it's clean. Making sure that there's a place for everything will make picking up easier and faster – and once you can easily keep it picked up and tidy, then your house will always look cleaner than it may actually be! [Cue the chorus of singing angels!] Plus, it can be quickly returned to that condition if things start to get a little messy. You can't "organize" clutter though. Having too much stuff will always make your home feel less organized, less kept up, and less clean. Basically, clutter makes you look like a much worse housekeeper than you may actually be. Don't worry though – there's a whole section on decluttering and organizing coming up! For now, let's talk about some ideas and hacks for actual *cleaning* around your home.

General Cleaning Hacks...

Most of us don't actually enjoy cleaning. (If you do, more power to you – and let me send you my address!) Unfortunately, it's a necessary evil, unless we want our homes to literally eat us alive. So, we're going to cover tips on what to use to clean, how to clean certain areas, how to make cleaning faster and easier, how to make it *not* feel like you're having to clean all the time (!!!) and all the tips and hacks in between!

Cleaning your home is just an unfortunate but necessary responsibility. There *are* ways to make a little more enjoyable though. Try pairing cleaning chores with listening to an audio book or your favorite podcast/YouTube channel, or while chatting on the phone with a friend/family. (This works for cooking as well.) Or just crank up your favorite playlist and sing/dance along while you work! This works in reverse too; if you're already talking on the phone while you're at home, why not get in the habit of doing some "mindless" tasks while you chat? Do a quick tidy-up, dust, put away clean dishes, do a quick-clean in a bathroom, sweep your kitchen/dining room, walk around wiping off all the counters in your home…the time will go by fast while you're chatting, and once you stop you'll have accomplished more than you realized (plus it will be that much

LESS that will need to get done later)! You can also reward yourself as extra motivation (example: "when I finish cleaning the kitchen, I can set a timer and spend 10 minutes on social media before I go shower").

So, what should you clean with? If you already have some preferred cleaners, use those! The most important tip though, no matter what product/item you're cleaning with, is to LET the cleaning products actually do their job and do the work for you! Most cleaning sprays are designed for you to let them sit for several minutes before wiping/scrubbing/rinsing them off so, unless you just prefer to get your workout by having to devote extra "elbow grease" to scrubbing your tub, etc., let them do their job. Sanitizing/antibacterial products work the best when they've had a chance to sit as well. If you've tried a cleaning product before and not been happy with how well it cleaned, there's a good chance it was because you didn't follow the exact directions and actually give it time to work! So, spray away and then *walk away* and let the product do its thing while you tidy up something else (or load dishes or whatever); then come back and wipe/rinse them as directed. Work smarter, not harder! If you don't have preferred cleaners or you find yourself running out, either go for multi-purpose products to keep things simpler for yourself or invest in cleaning cloths that are antibacterial without needing to use additional sprays/foams. Although investing in these may seem more expensive at first, they can provide significant savings in the long run since you won't have to keep replenishing your cleaning product supply. (Bonus – since they don't require chemicals to clean with, they're safe to hand your kids so that they can help with the cleaning no matter how young they are!)

No matter what you prefer to clean with, baking soda, white vinegar, Dawn dish soap, and hydrogen peroxide are all great to keep on hand all the time – there's bound to be a combination of those that works for whatever you need to clean! Peroxide, baking soda and Dawn dish soap will remove many stains; just sprinkle on baking soda, spray with peroxide, add a squirt of Dawn, and then scrub with toothbrush. You can also buy hydrogen peroxide in spray bottles (it has to stay in those thick, dark brown bottles to avoid light); this is great to use for disinfecting toys, bathroom handles, toothbrushes and more since it simply turns to water after it disinfects. [*Extra tip*: Have a stomach bug or other sickness in the house? Keep a spray bottle of hydrogen peroxide handy and regularly spray it on faucet knobs, door handles, toilet handles, and anything else you can think of to help avoid the spread of germs. Just stick to hard surfaces, as it may discolor cloths.]

If there are items that you're going to use in multiple rooms for cleaning, perhaps it will help you to have multiple bottles/sets of them! Try making a cleaning caddy for each main area of your home (plastic shower caddies work great for this). Having a set of cleaning items in the kitchen and each bathroom, for example, makes it that much easier and faster to be able to complete a small cleaning chore when you find yourself in that room/area with a minute or two to devote to a quick task.

Now for the most subjective question – WHEN AM I SUPPOSED TO GET ALL THIS CLEANING DONE?? If the way to do house cleaning chores that works best for you is to do a little bit each day, then make yourself a list and put it where you can easily see it each day. It takes the guesswork and memory space out of remembering what needs to get done – simply look at the list when you have a few minutes and see what you can do right then. Some people do best with sticking to a daily schedule (for example, Tuesday means you need to sweep floors and water your plants, and Thursdays are for cleaning bathrooms); other people will prefer to just have a general list of chores and mark things off as they get done, in no particular order.

Some tasks I will suggest are best handled daily. These include washing dishes, wiping off kitchen counters and dining surfaces, and spritzing a daily shower spray; there may be others that apply specifically to your home. Figure out what tasks need to be done every day in order for your home to run smoothly and not reach your personal "mess-stress-point" and make a list. If they're all tasks that you're already in the habit of completing daily, great! If there are some that you don't currently do daily but you know would benefit you, display your list somewhere as a reminder (where you'll easily see it multiple times a day) to help you get in the habit of addressing these items daily. Do the same process with tasks that should be completed weekly (roughly); if you want to assign certain chores to particular days, make your list accordingly. Display this one as well so that you can keep on track until it's an ingrained habit. This can serve the added function of making it easy for children (or others in the home) to know what chores need to be done each day that they can contribute to!

In addition to daily and weekly cleaning lists, spend a few minutes making a list of household chores or home maintenance items that don't need to be done weekly, but still need to get done (such as changing air filters, cleaning under the refrigerator, cleaning your dryer vent, etc.). Put the list somewhere you can easily access it but not have to see it all day (such as taped to the inside of a kitchen cabinet door), and check items off as you do them. You can just check off with a pencil so that it can be erased when you need to start over, or you can laminate the list (or put it inside a sheet protector or cheap picture frame) and use a dry erase marker. For monthly items, check them off as you do them that month, and then erase and start over the next month. For tasks that need to be done less frequently (quarterly or yearly), write the date that you did it so that you don't have to try to remember how long it's been. At the end of this chapter, you will find a sample list to get you started! You may need to add other tasks or remove some, depending on where you live, what kind of home you live in (apartment, 2-story home, townhouse, etc.), or other scenarios specific to you and your life. You can also include routine items that aren't related to home maintenance, such as scheduling medical checkups, vehicle maintenance, dealing with tax receipts, etc. The goal is to save you time and stress by not having to use mental space worrying about whether it's been too long since a task was done or not being able to remember if it was completed at all.

Try establishing small routines that will help break up the cleaning and maintenance of your home to keep it manageable. For example, I'm sure you've heard of Taco Tuesday (a personal favorite), but what about Toilets Tuesday? Each Tuesday morning, get up before the rest of your household and go squirt toilet bowl cleaner in each toilet in your house. Then when everyone gets up, make sure at least one person uses each toilet, so that they all get flushed after the cleaner has had time to sit a bit. Super easy, requires maybe one minute of your time, and keeps the toilets from getting nasty in between good scrubbings! Maybe you can initiate Sink Sundays, when every sink in the house gets a quick cleaning the first time you're in that room for the day. Little routines like this make the cleaning caddies mentioned above come in extra handy, since you don't have to worry about finding yourself in the bathroom and then realizing you don't have any cleaning supplies with you and don't have time to go track them down (or you're afraid you'll get distracted and end up off-task if you leave the room to look for them). A great little routine to get in the habit of is doing "quick swipes" whenever you can. If you have a wet washcloth because you just finished giving a kid a bath, squeeze out the extra water and use the washcloth to do a quick wipe-down in that bathroom (counter, sink, faucets, top of toilet, edges of bathtub). The same concept works for kitchen counters, dining room tables, dusting, etc. When you find yourself in a room and have even just ONE minute to use, take care of a quick surface-cleaning task. This keeps the most noticeable portions of your house from ever getting really dirty, and over time this one little habit will help "clean enough" become the normal everyday state of your house. Not only does this make it easy to keep a fairly clean home, but it also helps the "real" (deep) cleaning go so much faster when you do it! Ever heard of compounding interest? A similar principle happens in your home too – once you are on top of keeping the kitchen clean and it takes minimal time to maintain each day, then soon you're able to get your living room to this point too. Then before you know it, your entire house can be tidy in 20 minutes (notice I said "tidy", not "spotless to where you could eat off the bathroom floors") and suddenly you realize you haven't felt overwhelmed by the state of your home in months!

If you're currently feeling overwhelmed with the state of your home though, start by focusing on one room at a time. Generally, starting with the kitchen is helpful (you know, for dishes and cooking and all that, since most of us like to eat every day). Plus, keeping counters and flat surfaces cleared off makes it easier and faster to clean and is proven to create less stress for you. After the kitchen is manageable, consider what room you tend to relax in or spend the most time in, and move to that one next. This way, you'll be able to enjoy visible progress even on days that you're not able to do much, because the rooms you spend the most time in will be under control. This is great for keeping momentum and motivation going too! Once you feel how much less-stressed you are in the rooms that you've tackled, you want to feel that way in every part of your home and are more motivated to make it happen.

If there's a certain chore that you always put off doing because you hate to do it or always think you "don't have time," then the next time you do it time yourself from start to finish. I'm serious – use the stopwatch on your smartphone. I bet it doesn't take as long as you thought! Now you know exactly how much time it takes to do that chore (such as wash dishes or clean your bathtub). If it's a five-minute task, put on 2 of your favorite songs to sing along with and you'll be done before they're finished! If it's something that usually takes you 15 minutes to do but today you only have 10 minutes to devote to it, set a timer and try to "beat the clock" to get it finished faster than usual. Even if you aren't able to finish entirely before you have to stop, you're still that much farther ahead. Something is always better than nothing, no matter how small the something is. Sometimes we have a tendency to subconsciously say "well I only have 10 minutes to spare, and that's not enough to clean the kitchen" - so we don't even start. If you focus instead on "what CAN I get done in those 10 minutes to make it better" though, then it's that much farther along when you're able to come back to it again. If you can get a room to look 75% better in 10 minutes, then focus on how good it makes you feel to have it be 75% better, rather than worrying about that last 25% to get it to "perfect." Many of us grew up hearing the phrase "if you can't do something right, then why do it" or "a job worth doing is worth doing right/well." Although these phrases were said with the best of intentions (of impressing upon us the importance of giving our best effort versus being lazy), their result may have missed the mark. "Doing it right" is too easily equated with doing a "perfect" job, rather than giving it our best effort *at that moment*. Perfection is hard, and our "best effort" can look different from day to day. Better is simple. Any progress at all when you're aiming for "better" means you've succeeded. Enjoy the win and let it propel you forward to more progress!

Another tip is to set rules for yourself that will counteract any "If You give a Mouse a Cookie" tendencies while you're cleaning/tidying up. If you know that you have a tendency to get distracted while you're trying to clean (ever spend hours "cleaning" only to find that it doesn't look like you accomplished anything, and you never finished an entire room or task?) then set a rule that you cannot leave the room that you're working on. If you're tidying or cleaning in the living room and you find an item that belongs in the bathroom, do NOT go take it to the bathroom if you're likely to end up being distracted by tasks that need to be done in the bathroom as well. (This is how "cleaning the living room" somehow turns into emptying your entire medicine cabinet, and an hour later your living room AND your bathroom are now still messy!) Instead, designate a spot to gather things that need to be taken to other rooms and assure yourself that you will disburse them AFTER you finish in the room you're focusing on. Keeping your focus can be a little easier if you're trying to accomplish a task that isn't room-specific (such as vacuuming your entire house) because you can use your cleaning props (vacuum, dust rag, whatever) in your hands as a visual and tactile reminder to keep yourself on task.

Before we move on to room/task-specific tips, there's another very important bad habit that you may potentially possess that needs to be nipped in the bud. Quit taking on things that should be family responsibilities all by yourself! If you live alone, then obviously this one doesn't really apply to you. If you don't though, then make sure that you're not the only person in the household who is contributing to maintaining the state of the home. Have a family meeting if necessary! While the specific "balance" of housework and division of labor within your home may depend on many different variable factors (who does/doesn't have other employment, the number and age of children in the home, etc.), I'm a firm believer that there is no situation where only one person should be the one doing all of the housework. Again, how you divide up labor/tasks is up to you and your family, but anyone who benefits by living in the home should be required to contribute to taking care of it. Delegate! Ask your family members to help with specific things, not just a general "you need to help with cleaning the house." Don't assume that someone else notices or thinks of the same things you do (especially if that someone else is of the opposite sex or a different age generation than you)! This is another reason that making the daily/weekly/monthly/quarterly house chore lists comes in handy. Sit down with the lists while discussing who will be responsible for certain tasks – not only will it be easier to keep everyone on the same page, but it may also be eye-opening for any members of the household who don't naturally think about all the different "invisible" chores that need to be done.

Kitchen/Dishes...

Now let's dig deeper into tips and tricks that are specific to certain chores or areas/rooms of your home – starting with the kitchen! Some of these will be short and sweet – but still impactful.

Run the dishwasher every day (or night), or at least anytime it is at least halfway full. Better to wake up to a dishwasher three-quarters full of clean dishes than to forget later in the day to run it, or end up with more dirty ones than will fit in it by the end of the day. Run the dishwasher twice if needed. (What?! Yes, really.) Don't have time to pre-scrub the dishes or check them all carefully if someone else loaded the dishwasher? Then don't – just run it twice. No one will care! (Side note about the dishwasher: if your biggest focus right now is saving money, then try to only run it when it's completely full, and only once; otherwise, wash them by hand. If you're most focused right now on saving time, then run it any time and any way you can!) Also see if your dishwasher has a light/express cycle – it will save time and money by not running as long (and since you probably prerinse your dishes, they generally won't need the longer cycle anyway). Love the convenience of your dishwasher, but you're trying to reduce your electric bill? Consider turning off the "heat dry" option, and just have a kitchen towel handy to dry off any excess water as you unload the clean dishes. [*Extra tip:* if you have children who take care of the dishes, this is a great way to have them learn to dry the dishes, plus it won't be costing YOU any extra time!]

Does it feel like there are far too many dirty dishes when you go to wash them compared to the number of people in your home? You're definitely not the first woman to encounter that problem. (I feel certain it started becoming a problem right around the time dishwashers were invented.) Don't worry, I am NOT about to tell you to ditch your dishwasher. <<*shudder*>> What I AM going to suggest though, is that perhaps you need to simplify your dishes. For some, this may mean simply decluttering them — if there are fewer dishes in the house to begin with, then there's a limit to how many dishes can get dirty before SOMEONE has to wash them! (Notice that I didn't say before *you* have to wash them.) Unless you have a very large family, most of whom are home all day, then chances are that once you get into the routine of having dishes get washed every night, you'll find that you truly don't need all the dishes that you own anyway. If you're unsure whether this will work for you (it would, I promise – but just in case you're not sold on the idea), try boxing up the ones you might consider getting rid of – if you go a full month without actually needing them, then out they go! If you decide that you do need to keep some of them after all, then no harm done. You can also try simplifying the dishes by making it easier to know which dishes belong to whom. This is a great concept particularly if you have multiple young children. One way to do this is to purchase inexpensive dishes that come in a variety of colors and assign one color to each person in the home. (If you do this, I highly suggest finding out what your color options are first and discussing it with the kids beforehand to head off any "I wanted that color" arguments before they start.). Not only does assigning a color to each person make it easier to tell who hasn't cleaned up their dishes after a meal, but it more than likely will also result in you still seeing that you have more dishes than you really need. How many "extras" you keep in your cabinets is completely up to you and what makes you feel the most comfortable and least stressed.

  Another great kitchen/dishes habit to start is that when you've just finished cooking a meal, do yourself a favor and wash (or at least rinse) the cooking pots/pans immediately and set them in the dishwasher. They will rinse off exponentially easier when the food is fresh, rather than waiting hours and having it be dried on and stuck. (But if you forget this one, there's a tip coming to help with dried, stuck-on food too.) It will make cleaning the kitchen after dinner seem quicker and easier too! In fact, when you're about to start cooking, try going ahead and filling your sink with warm soapy water – then as you use a mixing bowl, pan, etc. you can either wash it right away (and set it down to dry) or set it in the soapy water to soak so that it's quick and easy to either wash it or rinse it and put in the dishwasher before you even sit down to eat. Once you finish cooking, dish out everyone's plates/bowls and then immediately put leftovers in a container before you sit down to eat. Place any remaining dirty pots/pans into the soapy water before you sit down to eat too, and they'll be ready for a quick, easy wash once you're done. Makes doing the dishes and cleaning the kitchen after dinner a breeze! This also means that it's easier to make yourself clean up as soon as you're finished with dinner, rather than saving it for when you're wanting to get ready for bed.

When in doubt, start with doing the dishes. Don't put off dirty dishes! The longer you do, the exponentially longer they will take to tackle. Having them taken care of, on the other hand, will instantly help your kitchen (and therefore your house) *feel* cleaner and less cluttered.

Bathrooms...

Want to know my least-favorite part of the house to clean? You guessed it – and I bet there's a good chance that the bathroom is your most dreaded cleaning area too. Have no fear though, for there ARE some ways to make bathroom maintenance a little more palatable.

For your showers, keep a daily shower spray and a dish scrubber IN the shower. Coach everyone in your house (unless they're too young) to use the shower spray after each shower or bath. Use one that doesn't require rinsing, and all each person has to do is give it a few sprays before they hop out. For the dish scrubber, you can either just have one regular scrubbing sponge or you can keep one of those AND one that can be filled with dish soap in the shower. Use either one to give the shower walls a quick scrub once a week (or twice if you have hard water) and use the plain scrubbing sponge to give the shower/tub floor a quick wipe using your feet! It's quick and easy to do while you let your shampoo or conditioner work on your hair for a minute, and it helps keep the tub/shower from ever getting too dirty – thus drastically extending the amount of time you can wait between deep cleanings! For bathrooms that YOU don't routinely shower in, they should be cleaned either by or with the ones who bathe there. If you have children who are old enough to shower by themselves, they're old enough to learn to help upkeep the bathroom! If you have young children who still require help with bathing, these tasks can still be done quickly while you're in there with your kid – and having them see you do this will help instill in them that it's part of keeping the shower clean, so they'll already know what to do once they ARE old enough to be by themselves.

Another great "hack" is to keep packages of baby wipes or cleaning wipes (baby wipes are great for this, even if you don't have little kids) in each bathroom. Make it a habit to use each bathroom in your home at least once each day (use your master bathroom when you get up in the morning, a different one in the afternoon, and another before bed – depending on how many are in your home). The first time you use that bathroom for the day, grab a wipe or two and give the counter, sink, and top surfaces of the toilet a quick wipe down. This takes literally less than one minute. It's not the same as a deep clean, but it takes essentially no time and it helps ensure that the bathrooms can't get too grimy before the next time you DO deep clean them.

Laundry / Clothes...

The first question women usually have about laundry is "how do I stay on top of it?" This is one question whose answer definitely depends on some of the specifics of your home. If you live alone, or just you and one other person, you're likely not that stressed by laundry. If you have multiple people in the household though (especially including young children), then laundry may feel like the bane of your existence. So, how DO you stay on top of it? The answer starts off the same for everyone — routine. Exactly *what* routine works best for you, however, will be determined by how many people are in your home (and their ages), and how long they're physically IN your home every day.

For instance, if you have two kids who are school-aged and at school all day, they're NOT in lots of activities that involve specialty clothing (such as gymnastics or team sports), and you work outside of the home during the week — then most likely your laundry can sufficiently be handled by doing it once per week. This doesn't mean you have to do all the laundry in one day though! Your kids are old enough to do their own laundry – let them each keep a laundry hamper in their room for their clothes and assign them a day (the same day or separate ones) to do their laundry. You can also assign one of them the task of gathering and washing all the dirty towels and washcloths in the house and have the other one wash all the bed sheets. My kids do this and know that they have to get all their laundry chores done between Friday after school and Sunday before dinner – because they also know that Sunday evening is when Mom and Dad wash their own clothes. (We'll discuss more about laundry and kids later on too.)

In a different scenario though, let's say you have 3 kids, 2 of whom are still too young to attend school, several are in sports and/or dance activities during the week, one is potty-training, and you stay home during the day. This dynamic makes it more likely that trying to do laundry once a week will become overwhelming, especially when it comes to putting everything away once it's clean. So, in this case, doing either 1 load a day or designating certain days (Monday, Wednesday, and Saturday for example) as laundry days will probably be most helpful for you in keeping the laundry monster under control. If your family's laundry load requires doing a load a day (or close to it) and you work outside the home during the day, try either putting clothes in the washer before bed and then in the dryer in the morning or starting the washing machine before you leave in the morning and moving them to the dryer once you get home later in the day.

See if your washing machine has a "delayed start" setting. If so, you can set it up before you go to bed and schedule it to start early in the morning so that it will be done as soon as you get up – then clothes are washed and ready for you to put into the dryer first thing in the morning (and they didn't have to sit there wet for hours waiting on you)! While you're at it, check whether your washing machine has an express/light cycle (just like the tip for your dishwasher). Unless you're washing a load of items that are truly filthy, most clothes will wash just fine on a quick/express setting, in cold water, with all clothing types mixed together. (Don't come at me for that one.) Not only can this help you time-wise (since you're not having to wait 45+ minutes for a load to wash), but it also saves money since it uses less energy and will help your clothes last longer since they're not being worn out by repeated long, hot wash cycles (which wear out the fabric fibers faster). Another way to save money on laundry (and on clothes, by helping them last longer) is to hang most things up to dry, rather than putting them through the machine dryer. For items that you normally hang up in your closet, this costs you zero extra time – in fact, it actually saves you the time of having to put them in the dryer and then possibly dry some a second time if they sat too long and got wrinkled. For clothes that normally get put in drawers, this is one where YOU have to decide if it's more worth it to you on this task to save time (run them through the machine dryer and then toss into drawers) or money (hang dry and then pull off hangers to put into drawers). There's not a "wrong" answer here (or for anything else we discuss) – it's all about what helps improve things for YOUR highest stress points around your home.

If it's easier/necessary for you to wash a load of clothes each day (or close to it) and you wash all the day's clothes together (regardless of who they belong to), why not consider doing away with laundry baskets? Simply have everyone throw their dirty items straight into the washing machine as they're dirtied/worn, and then it's all ready for you to turn on at the end of the day. Now you don't have to see laundry hampers sitting all around the house! This can also help with clean items being put away too – set a firm rule for the household that clean laundry cannot be left piled somewhere, it must be put up where it goes. If there are no laundry hampers, then there's nowhere for kids to "hide" clean clothes that haven't been put away.

Speaking of putting laundry away… learn to fold or hang clothes and put them away right when they come out of the dryer. No, it's not fun. But it doesn't take any extra time (and if anything is actually faster) than folding them later after they've been sitting on your loveseat or bed for 2 days. Plus, it eliminates not only the pile of clothes on your loveseat or bed for 2 (err…6….14 days…), but also means no one in the house has to search for a certain item of clothing ("Mom, where's my XYZ shirt?") – if it's clean, it's already folded/hung and put away! If folding laundry is a problem, don't fold it. Simple! Seriously – who else cares if your laundry is put away folded?! Let kids toss their clothes in drawers, and if something ends up wrinkled you can throw it in the dryer for a few minutes with a damp hand towel or washcloth or a few ice cubes (or buy a bottle of Downy Wrinkle Releaser). It's okay, I promise. Unless they're under the age of maybe 3, your kids are perfectly capable of learning to put their own laundry away. Regardless of whether you work outside the home or not, you aren't doing them any good by doing it for them. They won't be living with you forever, so the more that you help normalize household responsibilities for them and teach them how to do things that need to be done, the better off they'll be in the long run.

When putting away clean laundry for little kids, try bundling their clothes into outfits so that everything is already paired together. It helps when they're getting dressed in the mornings, setting out clothes for the week, packing for a trip, or when someone else (such as a babysitter or other relative) is filling in to help. (Anyone else ever had Dad get the little one dressed for daycare, and you have no idea how/why those clothes were put together??) Plus, if you do this while putting away the clean laundry, you're only having to touch the clothes once (rather than go through them again on another day to pair together an outfit). If you have young toddlers who tend to want to empty out the clothes in their dresser, or they have a small bedroom that is also used for them to play in, consider whether keeping their clothes in another area might work better for you. Perhaps try storing their clothes in YOUR closet, and only keep a small basket in the top of their closet or an over-the-door organizer in their room to hold outfits for the current week.

Rather than hanging up clothes, consider just "dumping" them. I'm serious! No hanging or folding laundry will save you loads (pun intended) of time, and for most clothes (especially for kids) it's not even necessary. Put some dividers inside dresser drawers if needed to keep categories separated – shorts, t-shirts, socks, undies, pajamas, pants, etc. Or maybe you need to use bins or cubbies (think cube storage cubbies or the Trofast system bins from Ikea) for clothes instead! Not only does this cut down on time spent on laundry, but it also makes it infinitely easier for small children to be able to help with or completely handle their own clothes.

Next, stop the madness!!! The sock madness, that is. Have you ever wondered how such small items can drive you so crazy? Well, no more. Let each person in your house have socks that are all the same (for that person). If you have several kids who are close in age/size, give them each a different color or brand.

If all of Dad's socks are black, all of Mom's are white, all of Johnny's are white with gray toes, and all of Charli's are white with red stripes across the toes – then all your sock-matching problems are gone. You can tell which socks belong to who at a quick glance, and all the socks that belong to one person will match each other, so there's no need to try to match up pairs (they can all be tossed into a drawer). Have a problem with socks getting lost in the wash, or you "lose" one and find it weeks later clinging to the inside of a fitted sheet? Try using a washable garment bag – toss all the dirty socks into it, close it, and wash them while inside the bag. This is extra helpful for little baby and toddler socks since they're so tiny! (Speaking of socks, there's another potential sock "hack" later on in the Organization section of the book!)

The key to saving yourself time and your sanity is often just finding what "simple" means to you, so that you can simplify your life. With laundry, maybe using a different color hanger for each person (or putting colored tape on the hangers) for their laundry would help – it makes it much faster and easier for anyone (including young kids) to tell which clothes are theirs in order to put them away. Or maybe not hanging laundry at all and just tossing it into drawers/bins/cubbies is better for you! Think about WHY a certain task (such as laundry) fills you with dread, and then try to find a creative solution to change that scenario. It doesn't matter how anyone else in the world does their laundry (or anything else) – it matters what works for you and YOUR family and home the best.

Random little bits around the house…

- For food that's caked on to a casserole dish or pan, fill it with hot water and add a fabric softener sheet. Let it soak for awhile, then rinse out. The sheet helps release the stuck-on food from the pan! (Yes, the easier way is to try to make sure that food never gets a chance to get stuck on, but we're dealing with real life here. The best of intentions don't always pan out, right?)
- Baby wipes remove many stains as well, plus they're great for quick wipe downs (as mentioned above). Since they're also non-toxic (unlike Clorox or Lysol wipes), you can feel better about leaving packages in the cabinets of every bathroom in your house even if you have little ones. If you don't have little ones at home anymore, you can still buy them to keep around!
- Expo brand dry erase markers will help take permanent Sharpie marker off of most hard surfaces. (Moms of littles – you're welcome.)
- Dampen dish sponges and microwave them for 20 seconds to help kill germs in the sponge.
- Pledge will help take soap scum off a glass shower door.

- Use a lint roller to "dust" lampshades, tops of upholstered headboards, etc. They're not just handy for cleaning up your clothes!
- Get a stack of cheap washcloths or hand towels from Walmart or your local dollar store and use them in place of paper towels. This is especially great if you have young kids who make lots of messes! Simply grab one and use for cleanup, then toss either directly into the washing machine to get laundered with the next load or toss into a dirty hamper. They can be bleached as needed when stained, and they can save you a significant amount over buying hundreds of rolls of paper towels. Since they're cheap, once they get completely worn out you can toss them (or better yet, demote them to the garage for garage projects/cleanup) and not feel guilty!
- You've probably been throwing this item away without ever realizing the additional uses it can serve – the plastic bags that cereal comes in (inside of the box). Nope, not kidding – these can be used to put leftover meat in (even in the freezer) or to act as the dividing material between layers of cookies, hamburger patties, etc. There are numerous other uses for them too!
- If you have a baby or a young child who is not potty-trained (or still has night accidents), make their bed/crib in this order: mattress, mattress protector, sheet, 2nd mattress protector, 2nd sheet. This makes changing

bedding for a nighttime accident simple and much less disruptive for everyone's sleep! It's also a great hack to use if there's a stomach virus making its way through the household.

- Tired of smelly garbage cans? Try putting a few drops of essential oil on a cotton ball and putting it in your can *before* you put a garbage bag in. This helps keep there from being lingering odors even after you change the bag!
- Any time you grab a paper tower or rag to clean up a spill or wipe off something (like maybe a few drops of coffee spilled onto the counter), fold it over and take a few seconds to wipe off over surfaces around you (the rest of the counter, the edges of the sink, etc.) before you toss it away.
- Make it a habit to keep the front of your fridge naked. Keep items you want to have out (like the week's dinner menu) on the side of your fridge instead. Then if there's something super important and you clip it to the front of the fridge, it will definitely get your attention! This comes in particularly handy if you have young children in school, since they're bringing home papers almost every day. There will be no expectation for you to hang drawings or art projects on the front, so you'll be more likely to pay close attention to something like a permission slip or "special dress days this week" list when you DO put that on the front. (Also, dry erase

markers work great on white fridges – just write a note directly on the door! White dry erase marker work on black ones, and there's one for stainless too.)

Remember, these tips and ideas are not to suggest that you focus all your time and efforts on creating a tight-run, always spotless house — quite the opposite! Their purpose is to help you be able to be as efficient as possible with the time and money that you HAVE to devote to your household responsibilities and other "adulting chores", so that you can feel less stressed and have more time to ENJOY quality time with the people and activities that you love and actually make you happy. No one ever looks back on their life and wishes they'd kept a cleaner house (unless it was truly a sanitation/health issue), and you'll never regret time focused on your family. Use the tips and ideas in this book to help you do more of THAT, without feeling like clutter or overwhelm will threaten to take over.

Keep reasonable expectations! Sandwiches or cereal is fine for dinner once in awhile; the house doesn't need to be spotless, just uncluttered and "clean enough". When you have one of those long, crazy, exhausted, "I'm done" kind of days, declare it a "maintenance day." Take care of the daily non-negotiables that you've promised Future You (not leaving dirty dishes for the next day, for example) and don't worry about "negotiable" tasks (such as vacuuming or scrubbing tubs) for that day. All you need to do is whatever maintenance is necessary to not have your home end up worse than it started at the beginning of the day, and then give yourself grace for everything else. Sometimes not going backwards IS progress.

EVERY DAY	
Wash dishes	Clear and wipe counters
Clear and wipe table	Wipe off stove
Rinse sink	Sweep under table
Make beds	Dirty clothes in hampers
Put away blankets	Laundry/gym clothes
EVERY WEEK	
Clean showers, tubs & toilets	Empty bathroom cans (Tues.)
Mop & vacuum floors	Clear out leftovers (Tues.)
Bathroom counters, mirrors	Wash & change sheets
Dust a room	Go through mail
Sweep laundry room	Wash towels, kitchen rags, etc.
Sweep off porches	Wipe doorknobs, switches, etc.
EVERY MONTH	
Check food expiration dates	Clean fridge & freezers
Clean inside microwave	Vacuum couches
Wash blankets	Wash bathroom rugs
Clean washing machine	Clean dishwasher
Clean disposal	Change air filters
Dust light fixtures	Baseboards
Clean windows & blinds	Clean under furniture & fridge
Wipe down cabinet doors	Clean showerheads
Organize clothes drawers	Wipe down kitchen chairs
Organize and clean garage (if needed)	Clean tops of fridge & cabinets
Clean coffee maker	Toss pillows in dryer (15 min.)
Clean under beds	Organize pantry/freezer foods
Dust ceiling fans	File /organize papers
EVERY 3 MONTHS	
Clean out medicines & personal products	Go through clothes & shoes
Clean out closets, toys, etc.	Clean dryer vents
Drain washing machine	Wash window screens
Clean air vents	Change shower liner if needed
Check dates on spices & cooking staples	Clear & bleach AC condensate trap
EVERY YEAR	
Air duct cleaning	Chimney cleaned
Power wash outside	Outdoor maintenance

Chapter 4: So Much Stuff!!
Decluttering and Organizing

Let me ask you this: when you walk into your home, do you feel calm and at peace? Does the rest of your family? If your answer to both of those wasn't an easy, automatic "yes," would you like it to be? As mentioned in the chapter on cleaning, an uncluttered house automatically *feels* cleaner (regardless of whether it truly is or not). Research clearly shows that having an organized, uncluttered space also lowers your stress level and helps your home feel calmer. If this is a stress point for you, how do you get to that point though? It usually starts with decluttering. If you continue to be overwhelmed by your home getting messy or staying cluttered no matter how much you try to "organize" it, then organization isn't your problem – the amount of stuff in your home is. So, the solution is simple: get rid of more stuff! Chances are, 8 or 9 out of every 10 women reading this book has much more in their home than they truly need. In addition to helping your home feel and look better, decluttering also makes it easier to actually maintain the state of your home. Less stuff in the house equals less stuff to clean! It's simple math.

Having too much clutter in your home has even been shown to affect much more than just the physical state of your house. It can have negative impacts on your health, finances, focus and attention span, mental well-being, energy levels, productivity, sleep habits, relationships, temperament and more. For kids, being surrounded by clutter can lead to overwhelm, difficulty focusing (which in some children can seem to mimic Attention Deficit Disorder), trouble regulating their emotions, attention and behavior issues, experiencing "learned helplessness" and more – all such big, complicated emotions for young people that don't yet understand how to process or even recognize and articulate their feelings. Clutter promotes stress, and stress prompts your body to produce cortisol. Know what cortisol promotes? Telling your body to store extra fat around your midsection. Need any other reasons to agree that clutter is bad? (I don't know about you, but if anything in my home is going to tell my body to store extra fat, I'd prefer it was the ice cream in my freezer – not a pile of junk mail.)

I once heard that "clutter is just unmade decisions." This is so true! It's easy to keep things around because we "might" need them, or you haven't decided if you're going to use that yet, or you aren't sure if you really like that top you bought, or you "haven't had time" to clear out the kids' dressers of clothes that are two sizes too small, or… you get the idea. Most of the clutter around our house is either from unmade decisions like this that we haven't forced ourselves to address yet, or because we have an excess number of things and may not even realize it. There's a reason why this chapter came *after* the one on cleaning and tidying – once you no longer have piles of dirty dishes or laundry and everything is put where it should be, it's a lot easier to see what items you have WAY too many of (plastic kids' cups, I'm looking at you)! Ever open up the utility drawer in your kitchen [side note: quit calling it a "junk drawer" – that just subconsciously gives you permission to put JUNK in it!] and wonder why you have 17 pens (or twist-ties, or whatever) in it? Yep, we all have. The important thing is what you did *after* you had that thought – did you grab what you went looking for and then close the drawer? Or did you take the few extra seconds/steps to pull the excess ones out and toss them? So much of keeping our homes in check boils down to training ourselves (and others in the home) to recognize these opportunities and handle them right then. And yes, I'm calling them opportunities because that's what they are – they're a million little chances to be kind to yourself by spending 30 seconds dealing with this 1 thing right now, so that you don't end up overwhelmed by the HOURS it would take to deal with hundreds of these little tasks later.

While having me say that you need to get rid of stuff may seem scary or overwhelming, it doesn't need to be. There are plenty of ways to address unneeded clutter in your home without having to find an entire day/weekend/week to devote to it. You can make progress minutes at a time, and without making things look worse or messier in the process! So, how and where do you get started?

For the "where," there are two starting points that I suggest: the most visible high-traffic area in your home (such as your entryway or kitchen island) or the area that causes you the most daily stress (perhaps your dining room table, or your master bath). For some people, these two suggestions may both point to the same place. As to the how? The simple answer is: just get started. You do NOT have to wait until you can devote an entire day to this (because let's be realistic – when is that ever going to happen?); if you happen to have a large chunk of time when you want to focus on decluttering, great. Just ONE minute at a time (seriously) can make a lasting impact, though. Think of it as an ongoing process, much like getting into shape (physically). You may see faster results if you're able to devote an hour to exercising every day, but even 10 minutes of extra physical activity will add up and improve your health over time. It also has to be approached as a lifelong change in living habits. You wouldn't put in all the time and effort to get your body into better physical shape just to then revert to laying on the couch 24/7 after you'd reached your goal and expect to remain in shape. Right? The same principle applies to decluttering your house – it may take more effort at the beginning to get things under control, but then you still need to do what's necessary to maintain it. (Regular "clutter check-ups" if you will.)

We won't delve into huge detail on all the ins and outs of decluttering in this book (that would be a whole other book in itself), but I will go over some general ideas and processes to keep in mind (as well as some easy tips and "hacks" of course).

One of the biggest obstacles some people have when trying to declutter their home is the tie to money. While throwing out junk mail, expired items, etc. is a no-brainer, the decisions can get a little harder when it involves items that you spent money on and are still "useful." You may feel like you're wasting money if you get rid of such an item. You've already spent the money to buy the item though – keeping it when you don't actually need or use it any longer isn't going to "save" you money or get you your money back. The money you spent on it is gone – period. There's no point in beating yourself up and causing yourself unnecessary stress by keeping it around, taking up space and making you think about it or deal with it every time you see it, not to mention having to deal with the extra clutter that it creates. Every item that you store in your home is costing you something – the space to house it, the time to clean/maintain it, the mental energy to debate on when/if you'll ever use it (not to mention remembering you have it), etc. Is it really worth that cost? Does it add value to your life or serve you in a way that makes it worth the mental and physical "expense" to keep it? If not, then it needs to go. If you don't want to throw away something that is still perfectly "good," then bless someone else with it – give it to a friend or neighbor or donate it.

Keeping items that you "could" reuse later is often not worth their true cost. Example: gift bags. Yes, the most money-saving thing to do would be to save them to reuse them later (and if you have space to do this and it's not causing any issues for you, then feel free to carry on). However, if you have a pile or stash of gift bags taking up needed room in a closet, "saving them" is costing you the space to store them AND costing you the mental and emotional energy of seeing them every time you open that closet and dealing with them any time you want to clean it up. I know, a stash of gift bags may not sound like a big deal — but multiply it times every other kind of item like this in your house (that you save for later), and……you get the point. Personally, items like that are not worth the cost of keeping them in my home. I'll just spend $1 to get a new one when needed. (Ones you choose to clear out of your house can also be donated – again, blessing someone else!)

While we're on the subject of keeping things for "later," we need to have a little chat. Although I obviously don't know the particular circumstances of the relationships in your life, there's one individual that I'm going to go out on a limb and say that you need to break up with. I'm sorry, I know that it can be hard – trust me. But this relationship just really isn't that good for you! I only want the best for you. Honest. I really do hate to say it, but here goes – you need to break up with her. Your "Fantasy Future You." There, I said it. I know, I know – she's a wonderful person, she means well and wants the best for you too. She has a great heart; she eats nothing but healthy gourmet organic meals; she works out every day; she somehow has all this extra free time that she spends reading a new book each week, cooking every healthy meal she's saved on Pinterest, making Tik Tok worthy lunches every morning for her kids, volunteering at all the places, and making crafts that make Martha Stewart jealous; plus her house stays deep-cleaned 24/7, her new YouTube channel has half a million subscribers, and she's THISCLOSE to being featured on HGTV. I get it – she's awesome.

Here's the kicker though – she's not awesome for YOU. She's costing you money – by getting you to buy foods on a whim that you're realistically not going to eat, pay for memberships and subscriptions that you don't use and don't need, and order items that she assures you are going to be the key to solving all your so-called problems. She's wasting your time too. Most importantly though, and the main reason that she's got to go, is that she's undermining your sanity and increasing your stress. I know, I understand – you WANT her to be you (or you to be her, however that works). The thing is though, you already ARE awesome. And that Fantasy Future You is as air-brushed and photoshopped in your mind as your favorite photo filter.

Please hear my heart on this – I am by NO means saying you should give up on your dreams, or quit spending time on hobbies you enjoy, or any of that. Absolutely not. I'm also not suggesting that you shouldn't continually strive to improve yourself and your life (which is likely why you got this book). What I *am* suggesting is that you need to quit letting Fantasy Future You derail your mental, emotional, and financial health right now by essentially convincing you that Today You isn't good enough. If you've been thinking about making changes to your eating habits and focusing on your health more, that's great! Start with baby steps though – if, for example, you've decided to try a Vegan lifestyle, then maybe start with one new Vegan meal per week and work your way up from there, rather than diving in head-first and blowing your entire month's grocery budget at Trader Joe's on only a week's worth of food, only to discover that you're not sure what to do with most of it and don't like the first few things you try. The same concept applies to lots of lifestyle goals that we set for ourselves (eating healthier, exercising, etc.). While they are, of course, worthy goals that would be good for you in the long run, jumping into them with unrealistic expectations will only set yourself up for failure, along with most likely costing you financially and emotionally (when you feel like you've let down Fantasy Future You, or failed to live up to her expectations).

Fantasy Future You also tends to be unrealistic in her estimations of the time that you have available to devote to hobbies and other fun activities. If you enjoy crafting as a hobby, then having some craft materials on hand is expected, and can even be a great activity to do alongside your kids to bond (or by yourself as a stress reliever and form of self-care). But letting Fantasy Future You convince you to accumulate (using your hard-earned money) and store (using up valuable space in your home) more craft supplies than you'll realistically use in the next two years just because of some cute ideas she saw from a crafty YouTube influencer...?? All that does is create more stress and anxiety for you TODAY, because now you've blown money from your already-strained budget, you have more clutter to deal with in your house, and you feel guilt and disappointment every time you see the items that you're not using.

 I did NOT write this book to try to tell you that you should become Fantasy Future You. I wrote this book because Today You deserves to feel as calm, content and in-control of her life as possible, so that you can enjoy it more and feel like less of a slave to the logistical, mundane details. I also wrote it because society and social media have somehow collaborated to convince women that if you're not meeting the standard that Fantasy Future You seems to be setting, then you're falling short. And that, my dear friend, is a lie. Plain and simple. Fantasies (including Fantasy Future You) are, by definition, perfect. And we're not striving for perfect here, remember? The goal is progress, not perfection. We're developing habits and systems to make it simpler and easier for you to make "it" better (whether "it" is your time management, the tidiness of your home, your spending habits, etc.). Fantasies also aren't real. So, it's time to break up with Fantasy Future You. It's not you, it's her. You deserve better. You can wish her well, but it's time to focus on what Today You needs so that the REAL Future You can be set up for mental, emotional, and financial success.

 Along these same lines, have you ever heard the concept of a "silent to-do list?" It's the idea from author Fumio Sasaki that every single item in your home is "speaking" to you, sending you a silent message. Dirty dishes say, "come wash us," and our unmade bed screams, "make me," and the bills demand "pay me." Forgotten craft supplies say, "why haven't you started that project" and piles of photos and scrapbooking supplies mock "what happened to saying you were going to make baby books for all the kids?" Everything that we own is telling us something... clean me, fix me, use me, you spent too much on me, file me, you're a failure/quitter because you haven't touched me... and each little thing adds itself to a silent to-do list that eventually feels like it's going to crush us.

YOU have the power though to control the messages that your house sends you! Why keep unneeded items in your home that send you negative thoughts or make you feel bad?! I finally realized that the things I was hanging onto were a larger burden than they were worth. Pants that no longer fit were asking me when I was going to lose those last 10 pounds. The books gathering dust wondered why I hadn't read them yet. *Why keep "guilty clutter?"* Starting today, put your foot down and take control of your silent to-do list so that it turns into only helpful reminders and positive affirmations ("you've been doing so well on keeping up with XYZ!") instead of a daily source of subconscious stress. Getting rid of those items opened up space in my head as well as my home, and it will do the same for you. Rather than letting yourself see these things as signs of failure, shift your perspective and look at the act of giving them away as a form of self-care. You are doing this as an act of love toward

Future You, and you can also be blessing someone else in the process who may receive the items that are no longer working positively for you.

Ok, so a few more random tips to use while you're figuring out what to declutter....

Before you start to focus on decluttering, first make sure that the items you declutter have an easy way out – meaning that there's a specific method already set up for HOW they are going to leave your house (unless you're just throwing them in the trash). One way is to have a "donate box" - keep a cardboard box in an easily accessible place (such as the floor of a hall closet, or the trunk of your car) where you can drop it items to donate as you come across them. Don't want to use a cardboard box, or worried that other family members will see what's inside and take it back? Try having an extra garbage can or laundry hamper with a lid – keep a garbage bag in it, and once you're ready to go drop the items off then simply take the bag out, tie it shut and drop it off. Boom!

If you know that there are multiple ways/places that you'll be re-homing things to, you can even have multiple boxes or bins — a small box for random food items you end up with that you won't use, so that you can drop them at your local food bank or a Little Free Pantry; a box for children's books that you declutter, so that you can donate them to a teacher or go put them in a local Little Free Library near you; a box for items to donate to a women's shelter, humane society, etc.; a box or shelf where you put items that you've posted to sell (just be sure to keep track of how long they've been posted so that if they don't sell right away you can move them to a donate box later to get them out of your house); even perhaps a tote in the trunk of your car to keep items that belong to someone else (to return to friend, sister, etc.) so you always have the items available the next time you see that person. You can also see if your area has a local Buy Nothing group (check Facebook) – it's a great way to give away things you're decluttering and help out someone else (who can get an item they need for free) in the process. Look at it as a way of contributing to community recycling!

So now that you're ready to start, one great way to help determine what or how much of something to declutter (especially if you're new to decluttering) is what author Dana White calls the "container method." Wherever you normally would keep a certain category of items is their "container." The cabinet where you keep drinking glasses, or the hall closet where you keep coats, or the shelf that holds your shoes, or… - those are all "containers," and the number of items that comfortably *fits* in the container is your limit. No spillover allowed. If you have more makeup than what will fit in what is supposed to be your makeup drawer, then you need to declutter that category and cull out enough until it fits back in its "container." (Notice that I said what *comfortably* fits – saying that the things in your hall closet fit just because you can technically physically close the door doesn't count if it looks like Monica's hall closet in *Friends* and things are poised waiting to attack you and fall on your head when you open the door.)

If the items in your home are under control enough that the container method doesn't seem like the right fit for you, but you still need some help in making the decluttering decisions, perhaps try what I call the hanger method. You've likely heard the suggestion before to turn all your clothes hangers backwards and only turn them the regular way once you've worn that item – this way you can see at the end of a season/year which items of clothing you really don't wear and should get rid of. If you're thinking "yeah, yeah – I've already heard that one before" then let me ask you this: have you ever considered using the same concept for OTHER things around your home?? Not only does this work well with clothing (including your kids' clothes too), but you can also apply it to silverware/utensils in your kitchen (turn them backwards in the drawer), cups/glasses/mugs (turn them upside down), extra home décor (put them inside a basket or bin and only remove if you use them), makeup items…you get the idea. This is a great way to make decluttering decisions easier on yourself, because it removes the element of "well, I might use this for…" or "Oh, I'll remember that I have that now and use it when…" This makes it black and white. You did NOT use it, so out it goes.

The hanger method works great for kids' clothes, but what about the real space-stealing, mess-making culprit – their toys?! When decluttering kids' toys, the first rule is to keep what THEY actually play with the most. Don't keep certain items just because you like them or think they're great toys, or you *wish* your kids would play with them. (If we're not keeping stuff just for Fantasy Future You, your Fantasy Future Kids deserve the same treatment.) If your kids don't actually play with those items, then they're just needlessly taking up space and depriving another family of the opportunity to truly enjoy them. If your children are old enough, get them involved in the process! Explain (on their level) that having too much makes it harder for them to have room to enjoy the toys they really love. Talk through decisions with them and let them help you decide what should stay or go – and listen to their reasonings as they discuss it with you. You may be surprised to learn how they feel about certain items or what they like the most about others! Not only can participating in this process be beneficial for them for the rest of their lives, but it also provides a perfect opportunity for you to explain that items you declutter can be donated to families who are less fortunate and to kids who may not have any toys. While any time of year is great to go through this decluttering process, it can be extra timely before the holidays (or birthdays). It's a perfect time of year to discuss ways to help others who may be more in need than you are, AND it has the added benefit of helping to clear out some space in your home if other relatives may soon be gifting new items to your kids.

Speaking of holidays, if you change up décor in your home for different seasons or holidays, start training yourself to be mindful each time you're putting out new decorations (or packing up ones you're taking down) and see if there are some that you didn't use. Rather than leaving them in your storage tote to deal with next year, go take them to your donation box NOW – then there will be that much less clutter in your home and another "unmade decision" taken care of that won't have to affect your mental energy any longer (plus the decisions won't still be waiting around for you next year).

I'm not saying you need to become a minimalist. Just like having clutter doesn't make you a hoarder, simplifying and decluttering your home doesn't make you a minimalist. It just means you're learning that too much stuff in your house makes it too hard to maintain and keep things tidy (which causes you more stress) and makes it next to impossible to stay organized (which gives you more anxiety and costs you more money). Every single item in your home requires your attention and for you to maintain it (even if that's just keeping a space for it and remembering you have it), so the more stuff you have then the more attention your home requires of you, and the more time and effort it takes to keep it resembling clean. I don't want you to get rid of things that make you happy! What I *will* suggest though, is that you take a moment to reflect on whether that item truly does. I'm sure you've heard the phrase "money can't buy happiness." While technically true, that particular phrasing can sometimes (understandably) trigger those of us who've dealt with severe financial difficulties before (or currently) – because we will be the first ones to counter that trite quote with the sentiment that "it may not buy happiness, but it sure does solve a lot of problems." Also, money may not buy happiness, but it can provide options. Instead of using that cliché though, try pondering this one instead (I wish I could remember where I heard it, because it's much more to the actual point): "your happiness can't be bought in a store." There are going to be some items in your home that truly do make you happy – always keep those! Chances are though, many items taking up space in your home don't. Acknowledge that they may have filled a need at the time when you bought them, but they're no longer serving their purpose and they're causing you distress instead. It's time that they leave your home, and hopefully clearing them out will help prompt you to double-check your true motives or motivation the next time you're tempted to purchase another item to bring into your home.

Now, all of this deep discussion may have you feeling like the process of decluttering your house is going to be a long, drawn-out endeavor. It doesn't have to be! As I've said, if you do have large chunks of time to devote to tackling your clutter – great. But even if you never do, you can still get it done! Just like we talked about being able to maintain house cleaning with short little increments, it works for decluttering too. Have an extra 3 minutes while something is in the microwave? Go tackle the utility drawer in your kitchen. Stuck on hold for a phone call? Sort your pile of mail while you wait. Got 20 minutes left before dinner is finished cooking in the oven? See what you can clear out of the hall closet, or your kids' shoe pile. This doesn't have to be a huge undertaking, but it also won't be something that you do once and then you're done for good. Finding ways to add in "decluttering minutes" to your daily activities and routines will not only help you chip away at the piles threatening to overtake your home, but it will also help you instill new habits that will keep you from sliding backward and make maintaining the clutter-free simplicity of your home a breeze.

In addition, some decluttering opportunities will naturally present themselves. For example, when it's the end of a season and you go to put away those clothes (such as winter gear) until the next year, take a few minutes to see if there are any items that are likely to not be useful the next time around. Why bother storing them then? Don't forget about season-specific shoes as well. For kids especially, chances are that by the time that season comes the next year they will have outgrown the items they used during this season. So, unless they're going to be passed down to a younger sibling, then this is the time to utilize one of your "way out" systems and get them out of your house! Not only does this serve the purpose of keeping you from using space in your home to store things that no longer serve you, but it will also make it that much easier the next year to see what you need to replenish (such as pants for the kid who had a growth spurt).

If you're trying to declutter your entire house and find that you get distracted too easily while trying to tackle one area at a time (perhaps because when you go to bring an item to another room where it belongs, you get distracted by things there), maybe try handling a *category* instead of an area. For example, if your house has gotten trashed then grab a black garbage bag and walk around your entire house tossing every little piece of trash that you find into the bag. When you're done, go throw it away – see? It's better! Now, grab another bag or an empty cardboard box and walk around finding things within eyesight that you can easily decide to get rid of. Once the box/bag is full or you've walked the whole house (or you run out of time and need to stop), go throw it in the garbage or put it in your car to be dropped off for donation. Progress! While at first glance this idea might seem counter-intuitive to avoiding distractions, since you're going to walk through multiple rooms, the act of holding the garbage bag for trash or cardboard box for donations in your hand as you walk through the house can serve as a physical reminder to help keep your mind anchored on what your focus is supposed to be and keep you on task.

Reward yourself for progress too! If you finally tackled all the clothing in your house or the kids' out of control playroom, then you've earned some extra TV-binging time or a dinner out with friends. (Just don't "reward" yourself with something that will only become more clutter!). This helps perpetuate your motivation and keeps you from allowing your feelings or temporary lack of motivation to derail you and put you right back where you (unhappily) were before. Remember, we're focusing on progress and making things better. One of the best phrases

I've ever heard was "better is a blessing; perfection is paralyzing." This applies to pretty much everything in your home – cleaning, cooking, decluttering, organizing, etc. Take it to heart! Stop focusing on wishing that your home was perfect or thinking that someone else's is - be proud of the progress that you make, because every little bit makes things better.

Organization:

Once you have a handle on any clutter issues in your home, NOW you can focus more on organization. (Remember, you can't organize clutter!). The first rule to remember is this: it doesn't need to be Pinterest-worthy; it just needs to be functional! Those that know me know I love to make things look pretty, and I prefer eye-pleasing organization in my home. That's not what you need to focus on first though! Making it pretty or Pinterest-worthy is one of the last steps (if it's even something you care about), and if you jump ahead and try to worry about "pretty" organization at the beginning you're likely to just end up wasting money and making things more complicated for yourself. Don't buy any bins, baskets, etc. at first – instead, use what you have on hand (even if it's repurposing cardboard Amazon boxes or food boxes or washed-out metal cans). Figure out what categories, groupings, placement, systems, etc. work for you first. Once you feel like you have things organized, live with it for awhile so that you can see if you need to make any adjustments. This is the best time to really pay attention and notice if there are still any "pain points" or stressors related to your organization – do you find yourself constantly going to the "wrong" place for a certain item, or are family members having trouble with finding items that THEY need to access? Adjust. It's YOUR home, so things need to work for YOU and your family. When you're sure about how you want to organize everything, *then* you can begin slowly replacing with nicer containers if you want (and if you do, start with the most visible ones first and the ones YOU see the most). Let's work through all that with a bit more detail though…

Where do I put things?

The first step to organizing your home better is to decide *where* you're going to keep certain items. This may seem obvious to some people, but that's not always the case – it can be easy to unintentionally skip past this step because you jump right to trying to figure out how to "organize" the items where they currently are. What if that's not actually the best location for them in YOUR home though?

Think about how/when/where you use these things. Start with *where* you use a certain item or category. For example, let's say you have young kids who love to do arts and crafts, but you don't want them using glue, scissors, etc. in their bedroom or playroom unsupervised, so you always have the kids do those activities at the dining room table or kitchen island. Each time they want to paint, you get the supplies from the high shelf/cubby in their room and bring them to the dining room for craft time. Why not actually keep those items in a kitchen/island cabinet, or inside a buffet table in the dining room, rather than gathering them up and bringing them back and forth from another room each time?

Another great example for stopping to think about WHY you are doing something a certain way is socks. (I told you during the laundry discussion that there were still more sock "hacks" coming!) Where do you keep everyone's socks, especially kids? Most likely, the answer is automatically "in their bedroom with the rest of their clothes." Okay, but is that where all their shoes are kept too? And is that where they generally put ON their socks and shoes? If the answer to either of these questions is "no" (such as you keep shoes in a basket by your front door or in the mudroom), then I'll ask again – WHY do you store their socks in their bedroom? ("Well, because I've never really questioned where else to keep them or why you wouldn't keep them with their other clothes?") This is a great example of saving yourself time and aggravation by thinking outside the box (or in this case, the dresser). If you keep shoes in another part of the house and that's where everyone puts their shoes on in the mornings, then why not keep the socks there too?! This eliminates extra morning chaos from trying to herd everyone out the door, only to realize that a kid doesn't have socks on and someone has to run back to the bedroom to get them (which is an even bigger hassle if you have a 2-story house with the bedrooms upstairs)! If you have young children, having all the socks and shoes in one central place can make it so much easier to help ensure everyone gets theirs put on quickly and correctly, with minimum fuss or running around. A potential game changer, right?

Challenge any "I have this here because that's where it's *supposed to* go" tendencies. This is YOUR home and YOUR life, so it be designed in a way that serves YOU! Who cares where someone else would normally keep an item? Or where/how that was handled when you were the kid growing up? Keep things in whatever spot makes sense to and works for you, not where an outsider would think you *should* keep it. Should you have "rules" of where things go in your house? Absolutely yes – that way everyone in the home (yourself included) knows where an item belongs and can learn to keep putting it back there. Rules and routines like this are a large part of what helps a household run smoothly. What the rules *are* exactly, though, is up to you and your family.

What do I keep them in?

What you store your items in (aside from cabinets, drawers, etc.) mostly depends on what works best for you. In general, baskets and bins are your friend (especially when you have kids). They can be used on shelves, in cabinets, in closets, etc. and are great for keeping a category contained and separated. For example, rather than having a jumbled mess in the under-sink cabinet in a bathroom, divide and sort items into baskets of smaller categories like medicines, skincare/makeup, dental care, children's medicines, bath products, etc. A great way to help save money and make it easier to adjust your organization as life changes is to always buy the same color of organizing bins and containers (I personally prefer clear or white), rather than buying ones that match the color scheme of the room they're currently in (especially if you have small kids, since the theme and colors of their room are likely to change with age). This way, you're never limited to only being able to use them in that room (if color coordination is important to you)! As your family grows, grows up, moves, changes routines and schedules, etc., your organizational needs will change as well. Having containers that can be moved and repurposed anywhere in the house is a huge help. If the container is a stationary item (such as a drawer), keep in mind that you can use things like drawer dividers to create "sub-containers" for different categories within the same drawer.

Also, don't feel limited by what area/room/purpose an item was intended for – always think outside the box, especially if you're having trouble finding a solution for your situation. As just a few examples: magazine file holders can work great to keep items organized in your freezer; utensil drawer organizers work just as well in bathroom drawers to hold makeup, toothpaste, tweezers, etc.; and over-the-door shoe organizers…oh girl, there are endless uses for those! Over-the-door shoe organizers with clear pockets work for MANY things – inside a pantry door to hold water thermoses/cups or food seasoning packets; on a bedroom or playroom door for toys; in the bathroom for toiletries, rolled washcloths, and more. If you don't want to see hooks on the "outside" of the door, use command hooks on the inside of the door to hang the organizer from. Got little kids? Consider keeping one of these inside the entryway closet (or as close as you can to whatever door you typically leave from) and filling the pockets with extra diapers/wipes, changes of clothes, socks, spare shoes, hairbands/bows, a hairbrush, etc. This way when you're trying to herd everyone out the door and suddenly notice that one child hasn't put on socks/shoes yet, or needs their hair brushed, or somehow got something on their clothes since they got dressed, etc. – you can immediately address the issue and still get out the door quickly, rather than having to go back to their bedroom to change clothes/diapers, or to the bathroom to brush hair, or go track down socks, whatever. [Extra tip for those with small children who live in a two-story house: if your bedrooms are upstairs, try keeping sets of kids' toothbrushes and toothpaste in the upstairs AND downstairs bathrooms. This way there's a set upstairs or use when they're getting ready for bed, but there's also a set downstairs in case you're trying to shuffle everyone out the door and realize one forgot to brush their teeth – saves you the time and hassle of sending them back upstairs when you're in a hurry!]

On the subject of kids, here's a few more ideas for organizing kids' items. First, try using the same clear containers (with lids) for all of your kids' toys. This makes the containers easy to stack (such as inside a closet), makes it simpler to rotate out toys, allows you and the children to see what's in each container, AND simplifies the tidying up process since it's easy for the kids to pick up toys and quickly drop them in the container. For board games, card games and puzzles, zipper mesh bags are where it's at – you can cut out the picture of the puzzle and put it inside the bag for reference (or tape it to the outside), or do this with the instructions for a board game or card deck, and the bags take up significantly less space and widen your options for where you store them! This also makes these items easier to store once they're in "containers" that are all the same size and shape, rather than in a variety of boxes. Plus, it gives you more options on how/where you can store them (such as in a drawer or bin, where it wouldn't be realistic to stack boxes).

Another great area to get rid of bulky excess packaging is the kitchen. Decanting (taking items out of their original package/box and putting them into something else) isn't just for aesthetics. It can be an important space-saving and decluttering tool. Keeping the box of granola bars with only 2 bars left in it takes up more space in your pantry than just tossing those bars into a snack bin – plus it makes it harder to tell at a glance what you're running low on. Moving food items into other containers also allows you to mix/group different things together to save on space. One category we do this with in our pantry is snack items that the kids take in their school lunches – rather than keeping every type and flavor separate, one bin may contain several different flavors of crackers, and another holds various flavors and brands of granola and cereal bars.

Want a few more easy organization hacks for the kitchen?

- Use command hooks and file clips to hang things on the inside of cabinet doors: seasoning packets, measuring spoons, etc. The heavier duty command hooks can even be used to hold pot/pan lids on the inside of a cabinet door!
- Lazy Susan's and pull-out drawers can help make more efficient use of your space. They're not only for cabinets though – try using some in your refrigerator for condiments (on the lazy Susan) or use small stackable drawers for yogurt/jello cups, small produce, etc.
- Magazine file holders (in addition to being great for freezer organization as mentioned earlier) work well to hold boxes of foil, cling wrap, parchment paper, or paper lunch sacks.

One important note for kitchens (and the rest of your house): flat surfaces attract "stuff." It's just a fact of life. Whether it's a kitchen island, an entryway table, dining table, top of the dresser, countertops… clutter magnets, every one of them. Once you've decluttered what you can from your house and given the things that are left a home (i.e., designated spot or container), see if there are any areas that are still naturally gathering "stuff" out in the open (such as keys, wallets, mail, etc.). If you can't find another suitable area to create a home for those items (that will actually be used/maintained by your household), then don't fight it - create a home for them in that spot! Maybe put a little decorative basket on the counter for keys to be dropped in or hang a small tote bag near your entryway to house mail (making it easy for you to grab the tote and bring it with you to sort through the mail while you're going to be waiting in the car or at a doctor's office). Rather than fighting the fact that this is where people in the home naturally want to leave certain items, create an obvious "container" for them in that location – now you're not fighting against anyone else's tendencies or habits, but having them contained (even if just in a bowl) allows your mind to no longer see it as visual clutter every day. Everyone wins!

Making it work for you...

Sometimes it's the small details that make all the difference. Whether it's the last finishing touches on your organization or some new rules or routines to put in place to be sure it stays clutter-free, don't stop now in the process – finish things all the way so that they'll continue to work for you on making your life run smooth and easier!

Once you've figured out where you want to keep something and what you want to keep it in, it's time for the icing on the cake – labels! Labels, labels, labels. If you're currently rolling your eyes or thinking that this sounds too OCD for you, just bear with me. Even for things that you *know* that's where they go, labels act as a subconscious cue to your brain to put the item back there in its actual spot while it's in your hand. This means it's a subconscious cue to other members of your household too to do the same thing (wink, wink). In addition, if you're doing some decluttering and organizing around your home, chances are that you've moved some things (or at least put them in a different container). Adding labels will allow everyone in the house to be able to know that they're returning an item to the correct "home" and help reinforce new clutter-maintenance habits. The type of labeling you use may be dictated by the container, the area of your home it's in, or just the style you like – chalkboard labels, dry erase ones, adhesive words or stickers, clip-on labels, laminated tags…I could go on and on. The important thing is that you use what works for YOU! Labels don't need to be fancy either – plain white paper (or white adhesive file labels if you have them) and clear packing tape make cheap waterproof labels that are quick and simple to make and won't break your budget. When choosing/making labels though, I do recommend that you use temporary ones at first (such as sticky notes) until you're sure that you won't be doing much adjusting on your organization/locations anymore.

"Labels" don't necessarily even have to involve words. Perhaps they just have a small picture on them (we'll talk about that again while discussing kids' rooms). Sometimes a "label" is as simple as a color! If you have multiple children and color-coordinating things works well for you, use it whenever possible to simplify your daily life. Assign each kid a color and use it for all sorts of things – their set(s) of dishes, their towels/washcloth, their school/art supplies, their swim goggles, their sock bin, etc. This is especially useful for teaching young ones to learn to be responsible for taking care of and cleaning up their own items.

Once you've put in the time and effort to declutter and organize your home, the last thing you want is to turn around and find that it's regressed right back to the same condition that was driving you nuts before! The best way to combat this is to lay down some ground rules for the house (for you and everyone else in it). Consider what the stress points in your home (clutter-wise or organizationally) have historically been and use those as a starting point for "rules" or habits that would help avoid those conditions returning. One example is the "one in, one out" rule – if one of the major hurdles to overcome in your house is/was simply having too much stuff, then establish a household rule that bringing new items into the home requires that at least one existing item *leave*. This helps curb needless spending too, so it has the added bonus of giving you a financial benefit as well.

Perhaps you feel like your major stressors were instead related to things just ending up tossed haphazardly around the house, rather than staying organized. If that's the case, there are several simple habits you can encourage everyone in the home to adopt that will help curb this. One example is "don't drop it, deliver it!" Take the few extra steps or few extra seconds to put an item back in its actual "home," rather than just setting it down on your kitchen counter or wherever. Some people call this the

"5 second rule" (though realistically I say use 10 – if it will only take 10 extra steps or 10 extra seconds, then take it there NOW). These suggestions sound simple (and they are), but I promise you that it's the simple little changes like this that have the biggest impact over time!

Our brains love seeing progress (that's why we all love "before & after" photos). So, use this to your advantage! Checking off lists, starting with visible decluttering, doing some 5-minute cleanups, stacking prepped food in your freezer from batch cooking, etc. – they all give you visual evidence of your progress and hard work. If you're trying to do more decluttering, simplifying, or organizing around your house, make it a goal to do at least 1 thing each day. Clean out your makeup drawer; declutter chewed up toddler cups you don't use anymore; simplify your socks or underwear drawer. It doesn't matter how small; the point is that it helps you keep momentum, and each little step accomplished is a step further than you were before. It's progress! If you're skeptical about how much different 5-15 minutes can make, then the next time you're going to do a quick tidy-up or declutter take a "before" picture first. When your timer goes off, take an after. Then bask in the comparison and let it motivate you the next time you have 5 minutes to tackle something. It IS possible to have an organized, well-functioning, tidy home full of happy family members, without having to spend every waking minute working on it!

Chapter 5: Kickin' You-Know-What: Productivity Tips – Routines and Systems

If you read the title of this chapter and groaned because you don't think you're good at maintaining new routines, and "systems" sound like overkill, take a deep breath. A lot of what we've already discussed revolves around routines and systems, regardless of whether you call them that or not. This chapter covers a little more detail on some of them and offers some new ideas for alternative ones that may work for you. Remember, the goal is not to have a house that stays spotless 24/7 and a jam-packed schedule that runs like a well-oiled machine but leaves you exhausted and depleted. The goal is to use any of these strategies that will ultimately result in you having LESS stress and being able to MORE fully enjoy your life, rather than feel like your life is running YOU.

Never forget: your best is enough!! Your "100%" will look different day to day. No one does it all. We all have the same number of hours in the day (though even that is a little misleading, since some of us need more sleep to adequately function that others), and chances are that the list of things you wish/feel like you *should* be getting done is simply unrealistic. The friend you follow on Facebook and that mom you watch on Instagram don't do everything on your "list" every day either – I promise! So, give yourself grace. When you're exhausted, overwhelmed, or having a rough time, just do what you can and IT WILL BE ENOUGH. Throw away one piece of trash that you see. If that's all you can do, it's enough. Wipe off one counter or table surface. That's all you've got in you for today? It's enough. Don't let yourself be paralyzed by anxiety, depression, or overwhelm telling you that you can't handle doing "all of this." You don't have to. You only need to do something – anything will be enough. Always remember – we're going for progress and making things better. No perfection needed here.

So, first we'll look at some miscellaneous productivity tips and systems. Then we'll focus on routines and brainstorming other things that Current You can do to help reduce stress for Future You.

General Productivity Tips:

Let's start with something that many of us automatically think of when discussing productivity: technology. While there are times you should veer away from it (more on that later), the fact remains that we live in a very technological society so we might as well use it to our advantage. Anything that you can automate or set reminders for is that much less that you have to subconsciously worry about remembering on your own. Chances are that you have a smart phone – so use it! Set reminders on your phone's calendar for things like "pay the utility bill" or "schedule my yearly exam." Use your phone to keep a running task list or "brain dump", since you always have it with you.

Keep notes in your phone of things like your kids' shoe sizes and their teachers' favorite items, so that when you're in a store (or shopping online) and come across a great deal you'll be able to check and see if it's the right item or gift for what you need. You can share your notes app and calendar with your spouse; not only does this help keep everyone on the same page schedule-wise, but it can also be a fun way to give little "winks" to your spouse to let them know you're thinking of them during the day (such as putting "welcome home kiss" on the calendar for when they should be getting home). If you have something like an Alexa/Echo device in your home, use it to help manage grocery/shopping lists, ordering items, setting timers and reminders, helping you initiate routines (especially with kids – more on that later), and whatever else you can think of to take more off your plate.

Have you already thought to yourself "well I *would* be more productive, except that I have these tiny demanding little munchkins running around!?" I'm not going to lie to you, momma – productiveness as a mom (especially one with young kids) looks different. That does NOT mean that you are any less productive though! It just means that you have different pieces to work with to create your own unique, beautiful life. If you're really in the thick of it with kids keeping you busy, then even the smallest "hacks" can make a significant improvement in how frazzled or accomplished you feel. Brainstorm on what some of the common stress times are during the week, or some repeated annoyances. If you have active kids with lots of different activities going on (sports team practice, swimming lessons, park play dates, etc.), try keeping a separate tote bag prepped with the items needed for each one – a swimming bag with goggles, towels and sunscreen; a baseball practice tote with glove, baseball hat, cleats, etc; a park bag with a blanket, sunscreen, small truck to play with, baby wipes, etc. This keeps you prepared, plus it saves you time and the mental energy of having to remember to transfer items between different bags or have to stop to think of when you last had XYZ and where you put it. If you're home all day with little ones who no longer nap, try having a set "quiet time" where they get to watch a cartoon or video, and you know that this is when you can either get some tasks done or have a few minutes of scheduled "me time." If brainstorming on your common stress points related to kids and schedules automatically brought to mind chaotic weekday mornings, there's hope on the way (in just a few paragraphs)!

Regardless of whether you have kids or not, chances are that you feel like your to-do list is never-ending. Am I right? Well, that's because it is. (What, not the answer you expected?) It's true though. There are numerous monotonous tasks that have to be done regularly – clean dishes always get dirtied again (just like clean kids and clean houses and clean cars), the bills always come again the next month, the food always gets eaten and needs to be replaced (much like the toilet paper) … the list literally does go on and on. Plus, then we have to add in all the occasional things, like doctor appointments and sports games and unexpected events. How are we supposed to make any headway on things, without running ourselves ragged??

Like many of the suggestions in this book, it's all about the little changes. One suggestion is to multitask. This may seem like a "duh" suggestion, but it's important that you do it the right way! Only multitask if at least one of the tasks you're doing is a mundane, routine "brainless" one. Feel free to chat with a friend on the phone while you wash dishes or clean the kitchen; but don't try to conduct a phone conversation while also helping a child with their spelling homework.

Trying to find some time to _____ (work out, meal plan, etc.)? Think outside the box. Even 20 minutes makes a big difference! Is there some time each week that you have to wait around (waiting at a kid's lesson or practice, or at a regular appointment)? Rather than mindlessly scrolling through social media (yeah, I see you), think about what you could accomplish with that time instead. Set yourself up for success - bring whatever materials you need with you, and even set a reminder alarm to go off on your phone so that you don't fall into the rut of the same old habit. Think that doesn't sound like it would make much of a difference (I mean really, how much could you really get done while you're sitting at a sports practice)? I'll let you in on a little secret – that's mainly how I wrote this book. No joke. As I've been writing this, I currently have one kid that has sports practice 3 times a week and another kid who has tutoring sessions twice a week. The tutoring sessions are shorter, so those usually get used for either exercise or for taking care of phone calls and emails (depending on what will relieve the most stress for me that day). The sports practices are longer so, unless I was working on something for my *actual* job (yep, I'm a working mom even without making this book), that's when I wrote large portions of this book.

What if you don't even have 10 or 20 minutes? Try 10 seconds. Learn to make the "10 second fix" a habit! Any time you open a cabinet, or walk into a room, etc. and you notice something out of place – take 10 seconds to fix it! Did a pair of scissors get left on the dining table? Take a few seconds to put them away in the utility drawer. Did you unpack a load of groceries and there's still a new tube of toothpaste waiting on the kitchen counter? Walk quickly to the bathroom and put it away. Chances are that most of these little tasks won't even take a full 10 seconds. If it's something that will take longer than however much time you have, you can make a note to come back to it later, or just address it the next time you clean that room. Reading this, you may not think that this is a "real" habit or something that will actually help you and your home. Over time though, little changes like this will help your home stay more organized on a daily basis and create less work for yourself when it's cleaning time! Training yourself to make it become second nature to use your *seconds* productively will lead to less overwhelm at home and give you more *hours* to use in a way that makes you happy, with zero guilt.

If you're worried that you won't know exactly what you should do when you have a few minutes to use, try keeping a notebook handy (or a note on your phone) with running lists of to-do tasks & other items. Keep it with you at all times and you'll have a quick reference to check and find something you can mark off your list on a moment's notice.

Obviously, lists are important (hence why I mention them a lot). What's even more important though is how you prioritize what you're going to spend your time on. There's a viral video you may have seen before where a professor is discussing this with his students. He begins by putting some golf balls into a clear jar, until they reach the top. When asked if the jar is full, the students unanimously say "yes." The professor nods, but then he pulls out a container of small pebbles and pours it into the jar, as the students all watch the pebbles trickle down between the golf balls, until the pebbles now also reach the top of the jar. When asked again if it's full, the students answer affirmatively. Without a word, the professor then picks up a small container of sand and pours it into the larger jar. The sand, of course, trickles through the golf balls and pebbles until the bottle of sand is empty. The professor taps the jar on the desk a few times to pack in the last of the sand and asks again if the jar is now finally full, and amidst a few chuckles the students nod and say "yes!" With a small smile, the professor pulls out a bottle of beer. Amid laughter, he slowly pours it into jar while the students all silently watch it fill the invisible spaces that were left. As more chuckles are heard, the professor points out that the reason his experiment worked is because of the order in which he added the items, starting with the largest. If he had started with the sand or pebbles first, not all of the golf balls would have been able to fit. In the ensuing silence, the professor explains to his now quiet, reflective students that the jar represents their lives and their time. The golf balls represent the core parts of their lives – their family, their faith, their friends, and their passion. The pebbles represent other slightly less important things, such as their jobs, hobbies, etc. The sand represents everything else – all the "small stuff." If the jar is filled with the small stuff first, there won't be enough room (or time) for the things that matter most. When asked about the beer, the professor smiles and says that it shows that no matter how busy or full your life is, there's always room for a beer with a friend. The moral of the story – what you choose to spend your time on matters.

Every "yes" to something is also a "no" to something else. Choose wisely. Don't confuse the small stuff for what's really important. At the end of the day, does it really matter if your kitchen counters are spotless? There's a lot of tips and hacks in here for helping you be more efficient with the small stuff so that it doesn't overwhelm and drown you – but don't lose sight of the fact that it's mostly small stuff.

Along those lines, try to include one item of self-care every day, and combine it with being outside whenever possible. Even if it's just standing with your bare feet in the grass for 5 minutes while you breathe quietly with your eyes closed, or listen to a favorite song or podcast, anything that helps to center and calm you is beneficial. Make sure though to choose self-care activities or items that don't counteract what you've been working toward. If you've been focusing on saving money, don't "treat" yourself in a way that undoes all your hard work! If you're stressed, rather than deciding to order take-out for dinner (which will just stress you out more later on due to finances), soak in a bath and listen to a great podcast. Nights like that are exactly why it's good to have ready-made meals or ones in your freezer that are ready to just pop into the oven/microwave.

What truly makes you happy? Focus on habits and routines that will help you be able to do more of *that*! Notice I didn't say to *buy* more of that. Without question, I can confidently assume that what makes you the happiest isn't a *thing* or item that you can buy at a store. Perhaps it's spending quality time with your family and friends, or traveling, or making amazing adventure memories with your kids – no matter what it is that makes you the happiest, it's likely not found in a retail store. So, institute whichever routines and systems will make the most difference in your life – remember, the whole point is to simplify and streamline the things that *need* to get done so that you have more time and energy for the things you *want* to do.

Systems Check...

Okay, now that we've warmed up a bit with some general productivity "hacks," let's get down and dirty with systems. (Not the best phrasing I guess, since the whole point of systems is to keep you from getting down and keep your house from getting too dirty! Just roll with it.) Systems are basically just the way you handle certain tasks or items whenever they come up (such as how/who washes and unloads the dishes). Routines, on the other hand, are a set of activities that you do in the same order and at roughly the same time every day. We'll cover those more later on in this chapter.

Having efficient systems in place for tasks that need to be done around your home is what helps things run smoothly and keeps everyone in the household on the same page about what needs to be done. Systems keep things from falling in the cracks and keep you from feeling like you've been spinning your wheels, running around like crazy all day but not having much to show for it. Saying that you have "systems" in your household can sound fancy (or maybe even intimidating). You already do though! I promise, you already have some systems in place in your home and your daily life, even if you don't think of them that way. Systems can be simple and cover small things like how you deal with text messages, or they can deal with larger categories like all the chores and maintenance tasks in your home.

Let's start with some suggestions of "small" systems that you can put in place. These are just a few examples, but hopefully they'll help you think of other tasks or situations that have historically been a stress point for you and prompt you to brainstorm ideas for new systems that you can implement to change that.

Something "small" that we all deal with multiple times a day are text messages. Bet you've never thought of your texts as something that you have a "system" for, right? While I'm not implying that all your texts require a system to handle, what about "spam" ones? Any time you get a text message that's not from an actual person that you know, take a second to see if it's something you need to continue receiving. If it's true "spam," this is an easy answer - your system can be to automatically take a second to block the number and delete the message. If it's from a store or website that you actually signed up to receive messages from though, often our default "response" is to either ignore it or read it and possibly get sucked into spending money that we didn't need to (or at the very least, spending time looking online at stuff we don't need, even if we don't make a purchase). Although it may sound counterintuitive to say that adding a new system to your life can actually simplify it, this is a perfect example. Instead of just ignoring the spam text (or email) or falling prey to its marketing, try implementing a new habit of spending a few seconds to reply "STOP" so that you won't receive them anymore. Seriously, it only takes about 2 seconds

– so why do we procrastinate doing this?!? Try to apply the same rule to emails as well, since they're almost as fast (though you do generally have to make a few clicks to "unsubscribe"). This simple action will now save you from the annoyance of continuing to receive messages you don't need (and having to continually waste time on them in the future) and assist you in curbing any frivolous spending habits. Not only have you simplified things for Future You by dealing with this once and for all, you've also helped maintain the peaceful clutter-free feeling that you've been working hard to promote in your home. You've taken an affirmative step by not perpetuating the popular modern cycle of purchasing things you don't need that only contribute to your stress level because they add yet another item to the count of things that you have to handle/clean/maintain and ultimately detract from the financial goals that you're working toward. Who knew that unsubscribing from a few texts or emails was that powerful?!

Another example of a system regarding emails is to set up a separate email account that is only given out to your kids' schools and teachers. I have one that is only used for things that may result in "junk" email coming (for times when you're required to enter an email address but don't want to give out your "good" one), one that is used only for schools/teachers/extracurricular activities and doctors' offices, and one that is for non-junk but not schools/doctors. This is also something that's great to do for high school students who are starting to need an email address for pre-college test scores, college and scholarship applications, etc. so that these important notifications don't get lost in the shuffle.

What about examples of small/simple systems that don't involve technology? How about this: keep an empty tote bag in the front of your car and a few empty plastic sacks in the console or glove compartment. When you're getting out of the car, grab any trash and put it into a grocery sack to immediately go throw away. If there are other items (not trash) that don't belong in the car, toss them all into the tote bag and bring it inside with you. [*Note:* when I say "you" here, that can also include your kids! Having them participate in just about anything mentioned in this book is just as beneficial for them as it is helpful for you!]. Then (and this is the key part!) when you go inside your house, walk around with the tote bag and spend the extra minute or two to *put everything away* exactly where it belongs right then. When you're done, simply place the empty tote bag with your purse to go back to the car with you when you leave the house again. This ensures that your car stays fairly clean, you're never embarrassed by the state of it if someone unexpectedly needs to ride with you or be in your car, and you don't get caught needing something while you're in the house and realizing it's out in the car (which is particularly not fun if the item is a jacket or umbrella and it's cold and raining outside).

Another great example (especially for those with multi-story homes that have bathrooms on each floor) is to keep a set of grooming necessities for kids in both bathrooms (toothbrushes, toothpaste, hairbrushes, hair ties/bows, hair gel, deodorant, diapers/wipes, etc.). This backup system avoids disruptions to your normal morning/leaving the house routine – if you're about to head out the door and realize a kid hasn't brushed their teeth or still needs to do their hair, you can address this quickly without having to trek back upstairs and risk losing control of your departure.

Hopefully these examples not only give you some ideas, but also reassure you that household "systems" don't have to be intimidating. It's just a fancy word that means you've found ways to be more efficient and productive with your time that work for YOU. What about broader-based systems though? Don't get me wrong, keeping a clean car as a mom is a miracle unto itself. Unfortunately, we tend to have a lot more demanding our attention and time than just that.

So, regarding your time, a perfect example of a system that works for many women is using time blocks or block scheduling. Remember the professor's example of the golf balls and sand in the jar? Using time blocks and scheduling go hand in hand with that. If you want to make sure that you get certain things done during the day that are important to you or are the most imperative to get done, then you need to schedule them or "block out" time to get those done first. Time blocks simply mean that you break up your day into chunks of time that are designated for certain tasks. For example, if you stay at home with kids, you might break your day up into blocks of time for breakfast and cleaning up, playtime/go to the park/outings, lunch and quiet/nap time (and you can decide what you're going to do while the kids have quiet time), errands/chores/calls, activities, dinner prep, dinner, bedtime routines, evening reset, etc. If you work outside the home, then obviously some of this "blocking" is already done for you since you have set hours to be at work. And if you're reading all this and thinking "well this isn't a new idea, I already pretty much do this" then SEE – you're more ahead of the game than you thought, because you already have a time management system, whether you realized it or not! The magic that comes from time block scheduling is two-fold: first, it helps you keep your focus on what you're currently doing without feeling guilty (that you haven't called yet to make the dentist appointment, for example) because you know that the other tasks will be handled when it's time for that "block."

The rest of the magic comes from holding yourself to the block schedule when the current time chunk *ends* and moving on to what you're supposed to be focusing on next. If you just gave all your appropriate attention to picking up and tidying the house, doing dishes, etc. for the last hour (or whatever the time chunk was), then you can feel zero guilt in stopping where you are at the end of that block and taking your kids to the park or playing a game with them. You gave your focus to that task during its allotted time, so you're free to move on – regardless of whether you finished it "all" or not. Any progress is better, remember? Progress over perfection. Maintenance over "must do it all."

Some household systems are extremely popular and can have a huge impact on keeping your home at "maintenance level" without having you feel overwhelmed. Ever heard of chore charts? Yep, we're going there. I'm not just talking about the ones for kids though – any schedule or list of household chores and who is responsible for what/when counts as a system. As with most everything in this book, the whole point is to figure out what works best for you and your family so that it can help things to stay manageable and not pile up or get out of control. Again, this isn't a "one size fits all" book – it's a "find the size that fits you best." Only you know what tasks your kids are capable of with their sizes and ages (though they're often capable of a lot more at a younger age than you might think), what your family's daily/weekly schedule looks like, what maintenance/cleaning items are specific to your home due to its size and features, etc.

The key is making sure that everyone in the home is on the same page as to what's expected of each person (and it's always better if it's written down). Want a few specific ideas? Refer back to the cleaning chapters earlier in the book (as well as the home maintenance list at the end) to see what items you may want to add to someone's current list of responsibilities. Perhaps you want to have certain tasks always be done by the same person, whereas others may change hands each week/month. (For more specific tips and ideas on handling household chores and kids, we'll circle back to this in the chapter on parenting tips.) However, your family decides to handle chores, that's your system (whether you realized you had one or not)!

One of my absolute favorite systems is really a cross between a system and a routine (so it's the perfect segue to moving into discussing routines next). I call it the Sunday System. My Sunday System involves several different routines that I go through each Sunday (yeah yeah, it's basically a series of routines, but "Sunday System" has a better ring to it). Sunday afternoons are generally when I decide on my meal plan for the week. Although I typically keep a plan (in my "everything notebook") for our dinners that goes several weeks out, each Sunday afternoon I look to see whether I need to change any of them (due to schedule changes, etc.) and then I write the dinners for the coming week on the wipe-off page that's kept on the side of our refrigerator. Even though I have them on the paper calendar that I keep in my notebook, keeping the current week's dinner plans on the refrigerator makes it visible to everyone and is a quick reference point each evening to see if I need to take any items out to thaw, etc. The next point in my Sunday System is to go through my paper basket. This doesn't have to be an actual basket (in my house the top shelf in my entryway locker is currently my designated "paper basket") – it's simply a designated spot where you keep any mail that needs to be dealt with, school papers that came home at the end of the past week to be signed/completed, etc. I grab everything in the "basket" and sit down with it. Bills that need to be paid are either paid right then (online) or they get clipped to my wallet in my purse so that they'll get paid in the next day or two. School papers are signed and returned to backpacks. Items that require an action from me other than paying a bill (such as making a phone call or email) are either handled right then (if it's an email) or they're put in my Everything Notebook and *I write down/mark a time in my schedule* right then for when it will be taken care of.

The next part of my Sunday System is to give myself a "preview" of the coming week. This involves looking at my calendar, our family calendar, any school events, etc. to see what we have going on for the upcoming days so that I can adjust my thoughts on dinners, outfits, other plans, etc. accordingly. If at all possible, I try to get this done before anyone in the house has gone to bed so that we can all be aware of what will be going on. This is also when I check the weather forecast for the week (such as it is, even though in my area it seems to change every few hours). This then presents the perfect opportunity for me to prompt our kids to prep their clothes for the week (if they haven't already). Everyone (even adults) can benefit from taking a few minutes each Sunday to figure out their clothes for the upcoming week in advance. Our kids are so used to this being part of the Sunday System that often when I mention it, they've already taken care of this when they were putting away their clean clothes earlier in the weekend. (If that's the case, I just ask what types of clothes they prepared for certain days if it's a time of year where the seasons are transitioning and the weather is even less predictable than normal.). Since all of our kids are in school, they each have a small 5-drawer cart in their room/closet and each Sunday they fill them with 5 days' worth of clothes for the school week. This makes our morning time go so much smoother (more on that coming up)! Since they prefer to bring their own school lunch, they also prep their lunches for the week with any non-refrigerated items they want. This means that each morning they only have to add the cold items into the lunch that's already prepped and then put it in their backpack (sometimes this is done the night before too so that the next day's lunch is totally ready to go).

The last part of my Sunday System is that I try to incorporate some extra "mindset time." This might be doing a devotional, reading a chapter in a positive book I'm in the middle of, or really anything that will help me launch into the upcoming week with a good frame of mind. Once the Sunday System routine is complete, it's on to my usual evening routine.

It's all just routine…

"What you do *every day* matters more than what you do *once in a while.*" – Gretchen Rubin

First off, don't let the word "routine" scare you away if it sounds too rigid. While there are documented benefits to doing certain things at the same time each day, there are exceptions to (almost) every rule and some people either feel too constrained by a strict routine or feel like they've failed and should just throw in the towel if they "mess it up" sometimes. If you prefer a more fluid daily lifestyle (or just feel like your current phase of life is too unpredictable for a set routine), keep an open mind through this section anyway. As with everything else, you can choose what works for you – but I'm willing to bet that there are some routine suggestions here that would be beneficial for you and your household.

Implementing routines in your home can make a significant difference in decreasing feelings of overwhelm, chaos, and frustration. It can also help set you *and* your kids up for success by establishing expectations and boundaries and encouraging personal accountability. Much like disciplining or parenting your children though, it is much more effective when done with consistency.

Establishing daily routines (morning, afternoon/after-work, and pre-bedtime especially) can give you a stronger feeling of control over how your daily life runs and improve your daily stress points. While you're reading through the upcoming suggestions, keep a list of ones that resonate with you. Write down your new routines so that you can easily reference them until they become second nature. If you need to, work on them 1 or 2 habits/pieces at a time (for each time of day) so that you're not setting yourself up for disappointment by trying to change too much at once.

Think about whether you're naturally a morning or night person, and plan accordingly. If you're most productive first thing in the morning, use that time for your important tasks for that day and give yourself a shorter, simpler evening routine. If you're not one of those "bright-eyed and bushy-tailed" people (night owls unite, am I right?!), consider having your devotional time in the morning (if you're home and that's something you want to do daily) since it won't require as much focus or productive thinking. Remember at the beginning of the book where I mentioned Morning You, Current You, Evening You and Future You? This is one of those areas where that comes into play. If you're a morning person, then give more tasks to Morning You than Evening You (and vice versa).

As you may have guessed, I personally am a night person. Decades of early-morning jobs and early rising children may have finally affected my internal alarm clock enough that it wakes me up early whether I want to or not, but they have had very little effect on the fact that I'm still naturally a night owl. My brain doesn't even think in complete sentences before 5 am, but large portions of this book were written after 9 pm. So, I honor my body's natural rhythm as much as possible and give myself a short morning routine with only the items that matter most; everything else is saved for the end of the day.

Obviously, you can establish routines for anything that you want and any time of day. (An after-school routine is helpful with school-age kids, for instance.) We're mostly going to focus on tips for morning and evening routines though, simply because those are the ones that stand to make the most impact on your day and your house. Similarly, you may have routines already at your job (maybe you turn on your computer, then check your calendar, then start responding to emails), but since we're here to improve your home life then we'll focus mainly on house-related habits.

Try thinking of it this way: treat your home like it's a shop and you're the shopkeeper. You're responsible for opening and closing up the shop each day. Morning You "opens" in the morning when you get up by completing the opening tasks that you choose for your home (i.e., unload clean dishes from the dishwasher, open window blinds, start dinner task such as putting food into a slow cooker, etc.). At the end of the day, Evening You closes up shop by ensuring that the dishwasher is loaded and set to run, items that must be handwashed are washed and put away, coffee pot is ready and programmed to start in the morning, counters and sinks are empty and clean, crumbs have been wiped off the dining table, etc. If Evening Me skimps out on closing duties, Morning Me gets annoyed that there are crumbs still on the table or dirty dishes on the counter when she goes to prepare breakfast the next morning.

As mentioned above, consistency is an important part of effective routines. It's particularly crucial when you're trying to implement new ones since the consistency is what helps instill habits. If you're wanting to make some changes to what your morning and evening routines currently consist of (or don't), try setting alarms and reminders on your phone to prompt you until the new habits become ingrained. Also (especially when the routines are new), do your best to keep them the same each day (even on weekends). Special circumstances may arise occasionally (someone is sick or there's an office holiday party to attend), but I think you'll soon find that the peace and benefits that the routines bring to your day far outweigh the cost of a few extra minutes spent completing them.

As mentioned above, writing down the routines that you're aiming for is a great way to help you create some new habits. Writing itself can also be a useful "hack" to include in several of your routines as well! Keep a notebook AND a pad of paper on your nightstand (and a pen, otherwise the first two aren't much help). Don't cheat and use your phone (your brain doesn't work the same way with typing things on your phone as it does with physically writing them down on paper). Well, we'll compromise – if you insist on using your phone, it can be used in place of the pad of paper, but you still need a notebook too. The pad/phone is to "brain dump" before you go to bed, so you won't be laying there worried that you're going to forget XYZ on your "to do" list. If you jot down "call to schedule dentist appointments," then your brain knows that you no longer have to worry about forgetting this, so you can go to sleep. The notebook, on the other hand, is for when you wake up. As soon as you're up, take 2 minutes and write in your notebook the things you woke up grateful for, your intentions and goals for the day, and your strengths that you're going to focus on today.

Lastly, before we move on to more specific routine tips, one of the best things you can add to a daily routine to improve your physical AND mental health is exercise. Yeah yeah, to some of us that's an ugly word. I'm not suggesting you need to join the 4 am crew at your local gym. If you're a morning person and *want* to do that, please do! It will be great for your productivity and your mental well-being throughout the day. If, however, you'd personally rather volunteer to be audited by the IRS or give birth to an entire football team without drugs than drag yourself to a gym while the sun's still snoring – I got you. Yes, research unequivocally shows that the #1 best way to move stress and anxiety out of your body is through exercise. Exercise is just *movement* though! You don't need a gym if that's not your thing. You'll get some movement while cleaning, decluttering, etc., but you can also find ways to make it fun. Turn up some music and dance while you vacuum or do laundry! Rather than sitting on the couch, pace around while you talk on the phone (and while you're at it, walk around putting away anything you notice that's out of place). Try to give yourself some movement time outside too if possible. Just remember one of our main principles – even a little bit of progress is better!

Morning routines:

Let's look next at some specific tips and suggestions for morning routines. If you're one of the morning people, this is literally your time to rise and shine! Having a solid morning routine will boost your productivity and increase your feelings of accomplishment and control for the entire day. For my night people, having a short but effective morning routine will help your day get rolling smoothly until your brain finishes waking up.

The time that you start your day doesn't matter, just that you get enough sleep and that you get up with ample time for your morning routine. Nothing starts the day off wrong quite like starting off behind the 8 ball and being in a frenzied rush until you run out the door. If you feel like you need to adjust your morning routine to start getting up earlier, start small – move your alarm 15 minutes earlier at first, then wait a few days before adjusting it another 15 minutes earlier, etc. Start with the morning routine items that most appeal to you, and then as you work on getting up earlier you can add in other habits.

HOW you start your day is 1,000 times more important than WHEN you start it. It sets the tone for your day, for your mood, and will even affect the mood and tone of everyone else who lives with you. So, don't hit the snooze button!!! Sorry, but yes – I said it. Trust me, it pains me to say this, and I fought it for years myself. Like it or not though, the truth is that you're not going to get a magical power nap in those extra 9 minutes that will make the difference in how rested you are for the day — in fact, it's quite the opposite. After hitting the snooze button, you'll still feel just as tired as the first time your alarm went off AND now you've made yourself feel rushed because you have less time to accomplish your morning tasks to start your day. If you're a snooze-lover like I once was, let me suggest that this be the first morning habit that you work on. Try starting with the 5 Second Rule. In her book "The 5 Second Rule", author Mel Robbins suggests that as soon as your alarm sounds, try saying a countdown in your head ("5...4...3...2...1") and then GET UP. No snooze button – just get up and start moving. (If you need an extra push, put your phone or alarm clock on the other side of your bedroom until it's no longer such a struggle. Just no getting back in bed once you had to jump out to shut up the alarm!)

Include items in your daily morning routine that will set the tone that you want for your day. If possible, get up before the rest of your household (or at least before your kids) so that you can have time to focus on yourself. Choose a few activities that will help your physical self – do some stretching or yoga, drink a full glass of water before you have any coffee (don't roast me for that one), take your vitamins, and wash your face. These will all help you wake up, get your blood flowing, and dust off the last of the sleepy brain cobwebs. Also be sure to include some habits in your morning routine that benefit your mental health. If you have time, sit and read something positive (such as a devotional or a good positive book) for at least 5-10 minutes, maybe while drinking your coffee; if that's not feasible, listen to something (whether music or a podcast) that is positive and uplifting. You can also have some morning meditation if that's more your speed. As mentioned above, start off your day by writing in your notebook or journal what you woke up most grateful for and what you're looking forward to the most that day. Also write down the goals that you are claiming for yourself for that day – start the day with achievement in mind! This is a great time to write out a few positive affirmations for yourself as well. How you start your morning and the thoughts that you start it *with* have a huge impact on your state of mind, your productivity, and basically how your entire day can go!

Get dressed, even if you won't be leaving your house. Research shows that this subconsciously cues your brain to know that it's time to shift gears from rest mode to DOING mode. If the first activity on your agenda for the day is exercising, then put on your workout clothes (brain cue – time to move!) before you start any other tasks. Even if you're going to be staying home that day, get fully dressed into regular clothes (including shoes) so that your brain knows it's time to be productive and get moving. [Maybe you're like me and need this part spelled out too – "full clothes" includes a bra. Nothing tells my brain "it's not a lounge-around-on-the-couch day" like putting on a bra.]

Next up, make your bed. I know, I know – I wasn't convinced on this one at first either, but I (albeit reluctantly) became a believer. First, especially for those of us who *aren't* morning people, it stops your bed from silently enticing you to crawl back into it. Climbing into a neat bed at the end of the day feels great, but messing up what you just spent a few minutes making...not so much. Second, it immediately makes your bedroom look cleaner and feel more organized, regardless of the state of the rest of the room. Plus, it lets you start your day by already having completed a task, thus signaling to your brain that the day has begun and it's time to be productive. This helps you start building productive momentum at the very beginning of your morning that you can build on throughout the rest of the day.

Incorporate going outside into your morning if it's possible. Connecting with nature helps you start your day feeling both centered and energized. Stand in the grass and take deep breaths as you stretch. Try sitting on your patio to drink your coffee and do your devotional or reading. If you can't go outside, think creatively on how to connect with the outdoors as you start your day – even if it means something as simple as opening the blinds and sitting near a window with the best morning view while you complete a task or two.

When you're ready to start your main activities for the day, start with your "frog." Brian Tracy, author of "Eat the Frog", goes in depth into the vast benefits that come with tackling the most difficult or dreaded item on your to-do list first. The difference that doing this will make in your productivity for the entire day is truly astounding. Is it fun? Usually not. Does it exponentially increase the chances of you actually having more time that day for stuff that IS fun than if you didn't start with your "frog?" Absolutely. Once the biggest, hairiest issue has been dealt with first, you'll likely sail through your other tasks for the day smoothly and faster than if you had wasted time and brain power creatively procrastinating and allowing yourself to be distracted by doing everything other than *that*.

While I'm on a roll with giving out the ill-received tips…No looking at your phone until your morning routine is complete! Better yet, leave it alone until after you've completed your "frog" task if possible. (Lost you now, didn't I?) Trust me, I get it. I know how tempting it is to start the day off with something "easy" like scrolling on social media. "Oh, I'm just going to look for a few minutes before I <u>(fill in the blank)</u>." The problem is, it rarely lasts only a few minutes, and you know it. Yes, I said at the beginning that this book is like chatting with your BFF over coffee (just with more brainstorming than venting) – but a true friend knows when some tough love is needed too. I could go into detail with listing all the reasons why that's not a good or productive thing to do early in the morning, but I'm pretty sure you can guess all of it yourself. If this tip is still a hard "nope" for you, then try this instead – if you *really* don't want to give up your morning social media, then set a timer on your phone. I'm serious! If your argument for including social media (or other phone activities) during what is arguably the most crucial part of your day is that you'll only do it for a few minutes, then set a timer on your phone before you start and *turn it off* when the timer ends. If your justification for it is that it's for your business, then only post what you need to for business and then put it away. Hear me out – I'm not saying to avoid the phone all day long, and I'm not even saying to stay away from it for the whole morning! But no one can say with a straight face that it's not a time-sucker, and I think the odds are really good that it's not related to any of the most important items or habits that are going to give you the best and strongest start to your day.

Okay, tough love is over (for now)! Let's switch gears to something that can be just plain tough – trying to establish new routines (especially in the morning) if you have young kids! If you do, do NOT get discouraged and give up on a new morning routine if you're trying to get up earlier and they unexpectedly start joining you. Yep, I've been there too. You decide to start getting up earlier and having a better morning routine, and then low and behold your toddler suddenly starts waking up an hour earlier than usual – right when you're trying to have some morning "me time!" If you've had this happen before and given up after a few days, try again. Give it time though! No matter how quiet you may try to be, the fact is that the ambient sounds in the house will be different than they were before when the whole house was still sleeping at that time. Their little brains are picking up on this, which signals them to get up. Gently redirect them to bed if possible; if not, just give it time. After a few weeks, they'll adjust to the noise change and go back to their usual waking time.

Speaking of little ones in the morning, create a morning routine for your kids too! Kids thrive with routine and well-defined expectations. Consider also including some morning "rules" that apply if they wake up early before you're finished with your own morning routine. Discuss activities that they're allowed to do on their own if they wake up early, such as reading or playing quietly with items in their room until you say it's time to start the day. If they're old enough, perhaps have some premade breakfast options that they can grab themselves if they wake extra early and are hungry. If you have children that leave the house every morning for school or daycare, set up a designated spot in the house (as close to the door you leave from as possible) to keep backpacks, jackets, daycare bags, lunch boxes, shoes and socks, etc. – everything you need to leave with on those mornings. If you have a mudroom or front coat closet or cubby, great. If you don't, then think outside the box and set something up! A cubby shelf or bookshelf and some hooks on the wall; some metal lockers (this is what we use); a shoe cabinet – whatever will work in your space so that you have a "landing zone" to put those items in when everyone arrives home at the end of the day and to easily grab them as you head out the door in the mornings. There's a good chance that your kids already *have* a morning routine, even if you've never called it that. (Eat breakfast…brush their teeth…get dressed…brush hair…get shoes on and ready to leave.) Regardless, it's never too late to start one! As I've suggested before for you, having it written out is a great way to have a visual reminder for kids as well of what they're supposed to be doing next. If they're too little to read, use pictures! If they're old enough to recognize pictures of a toothbrush, a pair of clothes, and shoes, then they're old enough to learn easily what the routine is. And if they *are* old enough to read, then they're definitely capable of completing a simple routine without needing constant urging from you (though they may need consistent reminders from you at first as they establish the habits).

Ready for an "extreme routine" idea? Sometimes when you're truly "in the weeds" and in a stressful phase of life (particularly if that phase involves multiple little kids to get out the door every day), you may need to temporarily utilize more extreme measures. For instance - let's say that you work outside the home, and you have several young kids to get ready each day, including a toddler who is REALLY not a morning person and requires lots of prodding and rushing for you to be able to leave on time in the mornings. Why not try letting him sleep in the clothes he needs to wear the next day?! Most young kids' clothes do not wrinkle that easily (and if they do – who's truly going to care?) – this allows you to not only save time and hassle in the morning, but also diffuse any outfit arguments the night before. (If you're worried about spills during breakfast or while brushing his teeth, add a loose extra t-shirt on top that you can pull off of him and be ready to walk out the door.) It may be unconventional, but if it makes your life easier and helps your day start out smoother and with less hassle, then it sounds like a winning idea to me!

As always, the goal is to figure out what works for YOU. There's no perfect cookie cutter routine that is exactly right for everyone. What's right for you in this stage of life may even likely be different than what works best for you years down the road, especially if you currently (or in the future) have little ones who wake up extremely early (or ones that wake throughout the night, since your sleep is also important). The habits that get included in YOUR morning routine should serve what you want to achieve, how you want to intentionally start your day, and what is most important to *you*. A good morning routine helps you start the day feeling in control, rather than being bounced around and running out the door in chaos, just to spend the rest of the day having to constantly react to whatever the day throws at you.

As you can see, the vast majority of the suggested morning routine tips revolve around being intentional with how you start your day and what activities you start it with. Take this a step further and be intentional about having positive interactions with your family first thing in the morning too – it helps set everyone's tone for their day!

Evening routines:

After a long day of chasing tornadoes, err…I mean toddlers, or of slaving away at the office and then coming home to do the dinner dance (feed 'em, bathe 'em, off to bed with 'em), the last thing you probably feel like doing is cleaning or tidying anything. Hear me out though! Even if you're more of a morning person than a night person, there are still reasons to have a solid evening routine. (And I don't mean a routine of binging Netflix and scrolling on social media in bed!) Your evening routine is just as crucial as your morning one. While the morning routine affects the tone of your day and where your mind is focused throughout the day, your evening routine can determine the quality of your sleep, your stress level, how centered and energetic you feel the next day…you catch my drift. Plus, it can determine how effective your morning routine is the next day – because if you skip the evening tasks, guess what's waiting to stare you in the face the next morning? Your evening routine is your chance to set the tone for how your day ends and set yourself up for success for tomorrow. Trying to do one without the other is just sabotaging yourself – much like having a protein shake for breakfast because you're trying to improve your health, and then eating an entire extra-large pizza for dinner.

Your evening routine is all about what Evening You can do to help tomorrow be as good as possible for Morning You and Future You. Evening You is closing up shop so that your home ends the day (and starts the next one) tidy, uncluttered and at peace. She's also doing a few small things to make life easier for Morning You because let's face it – for most moms, mornings are busier and more chaotic than nighttime. So, here's some suggestions of habits to incorporate into your evening rituals (or maybe to spark some ideas of other tasks you want to include that are specific to your life)!

Prepare your coffee pot and set its timer so that it will brew and have coffee ready and waiting for you when you get up in the morning! If yours isn't programmable, get everything ready so that all you'll have to do once you're up in the morning is push start. [A "next level tip": if you have medications or supplements to take in the morning and you have a hard time remembering to take them on time on hectic days, try starting a routine of putting the pill bottle inside the coffee mug you know you'll grab in the morning, or keep them on the same shelf as the coffee cups so that you'll be sure to see them in the morning – we all know you're not going to forget to make your coffee!]

Ten minutes spent at night to prepare for the next morning is worth its weight in gold! Get clothes, lunches, backpacks, errand items, etc. all ready before you go to bed. (If you have school-age kids, make this part of *their* evening routine too – they can prep their own backpacks, lunches, and clothes!) Look at your calendar or agenda for the next day to remind yourself of any appointments or necessary tasks so that you can ensure you're fully prepared for them. Put anything out-of-the-ordinary that you'll need the next day set out in advance.

Look at what your dinner plans are for tomorrow and do what you can to prepare (pull meat out to thaw or put everything in the slow cooker/InstantPot/casserole dish and just set it in the fridge, etc.). If you have time, consider cooking the meat the night before so that it's one less step you'll have to complete tomorrow evening.

One of the non-negotiable items in your evening routine should be a quick tidy-up. Even just 5 or 10 minutes spent picking up any mess and returning items left out to their correct "home" will help you wake up to a neater house, and help you start the next day feeling invigorated and accomplished (rather than feeling like you're starting the next day already running behind). Part of Evening You's "closing up shop" duties is to ensure that Tomorrow You isn't paying the price for today's activities (or laziness). A nightly reset of your home helps instill peace and ensures that the next day truly feels like a clean slate.

Make sure that your evening routine includes some self-care, no matter how simple it is. It will improve your well-being, as well as your state of mind as you try to enter dreamland. Have the last items in your evening routine be ones that promote relaxation and cue your body and mind that it's time to rest. Wash your face with warm water; do some gentle stretches to release tension that your muscles are holding from the day; anything that helps relax you for quality sleep. Grab your notebook/journal and write down what you were most thankful for today. If there are any reminders that you need to write to yourself for tasks for tomorrow, write them down so that you'll subconsciously know that they won't be forgotten. Just be sure that the last writing you do is focused on gratitude.

Once you're in bed, this can be a great time to read – but only an actual physical book! Okay, magazines can be acceptable too, but the main point is NO electronics! Yeah, I know, people are going to come at me for this one. Like it or not though, facts are facts. Social media is a time sucker, and the blue light from the screen on your phone (or tablet or whatever) stimulates your brain in a way that amps it up, rather than helping it wind down for the day. Plus, chances are good that you'll scroll past something that your brain wants to start thinking about and focusing on, rather than going to sleep. If your reaction to this "rule" is "but sometimes that's the only time I get to do that," then try this: give yourself an allotted amount of time after your kids' bedtime to play on your phone. Set a timer though! Then once the timer goes off, close out everything on your phone and move on to your evening routine.

Lastly, GO TO SLEEP! As tempting as it can be to spend "just a few more minutes" doing whatever, even natural night-owls need adequate sleep to function their best the next day. Studies show that most adults need 7-9 hours of sleep each night. Women in general, especially moms, are prone to being sleep deprived – and yet generally speaking, we need more sleep than men do to function at our best! While yes, it's important to have Evening You do things to help the next day get off to its best possible start for Morning You, be realistic AND pay attention to the time. Morning You won't appreciate a re-organized pantry because you were "on a roll" last night if it means she's extra tired due to Evening You going to bed 2 hours later than normal. Not only will an inadequate amount of sleep make it harder to get up on time the next morning and make your brain feel foggy all day (thus killing your productivity and your attention span), losing too much sleep over time can lead to bigger health issues. Reduced immune function, greater risk for obesity, greater risk for diabetes, poor diet, and an increased risk of issues such as depression and anxiety are just a few. It's not just "beauty sleep" – it's health sleep! Plus, being sleep-deprived tends to make you an overly-sensitive, emotional mess (every parent can testify to this with their kids – but it happens to us adults too).

Speaking of emotional, sleep-deprived kids, an evening routine for your children can be a game changer for everyone in the house. Kids thrive with routines. It helps establish household expectations, gives them a sense of control since they know what's coming, and (in the case of evening routines) helps cue their little brains that it's time to wind down and go to sleep. Have a family evening routine that occurs before the kids' bedtime. Try dimming the lights in your house an hour or two before bedtime. Since most of us are not literally rising and falling by the sun, it helps imitate dusk to signal your brain that it's time to wind down for the day. If you have an Alexa/Echo/something similar, you can also set alarms with it to have it gently announce reminders that it's time to pick up toys, time for baths, time to turn off all electronics, time for quiet/story time, time for bed, etc. An added benefit to doing this is that kids inherently won't try to argue as much with an alarm/Alexa as they may with you, if an evening routine is a new concept in your home. (This is often extra helpful for children with special needs that may cling extra hard to routines and cues.) Once routines and habits like this are established, you may be amazed at how much smoother and more peacefully their evenings go!

As mentioned before, when you're starting to implement new routines, it can help to use something (planner, phone app, sticky note on the fridge) to keep you from forgetting tasks and help keep you accountable to practicing your new habits so they stick. Recommend this book to a friend so you can compare notes of what you've tried and become accountability partners! Remember, establishing routines is all about making things easier for YOU. I'm not your mom. Ha! The only person who's going to be upset and fussing at you if you skip out on your routines is Future You. Now obviously, there are times that unexpected situations arise. If it's been an unusually hectic/late day or circumstances have you getting a later start than normal, get creative. Cut out any tasks that can be skipped without it feeling like a punishment to Tomorrow You. Delegate what you can – maybe you're usually the one who loads the dishwasher just because you like the way you do it best, but having someone else do it this time is better than it not getting done at all! Combine/modify tasks (example: instead of reading, listen to calming music while you wash your face) so that you can get your items done a little faster. No matter what though, keep in mind that the whole point is to make your life run smoother and more efficiently.

Routines and systems are definitely the backbone of a well-functioning, productive home. Fun and spontaneity are obviously important as well though – what's the point of simplifying and streamlining your life if you don't also leave time to enjoy and LIVE it? My advice here? Stop waiting. Don't wait for the "perfect date night" to wear that new top that makes you feel good – wear it now, even if it's just to the grocery store. Don't wait for a "better house" to fix up the way you want and invite people over — light some candles, grab some chips and salsa and paper plates, and fill that home with friends and laughter! Also, don't wait until you're in an "easier" phase of life to start tackling some of the things in this book. The more stressful and chaotic your life is, the more you *need* these right now!

Chapter 6: More Ways to Spend Less – Simple Budgeting Tips

If you're hyper-focused on your household budget and saving money right now so you decided to just skip to this chapter first…girl, you've missed a lot. If you've dutifully been reading the chapters in order, then you know we've already covered lots of ways you can ease some financial stress (especially with your food and grocery costs). The purpose of this short chapter then is to give some broader suggestions for your budget and financial stress points overall. It's a brief chapter because (a) we're not starting from scratch like how to balance a checkbook, (b) I'm not a fancy budget guru, I don't give financial advice, and there are plenty of amazing books and other resources out there to dig deeper into this subject, and (c) [most importantly] this book is about *simplifying* your life, so we're just going for simple, fairly generic tips. I think it's a pretty safe bet that most of you are like me – meaning that talking about budgets and looking at how much money you spend every month is about as enjoyable as going to a dental appointment or your annual gyno exam. Unfortunately, ensuring your financial health requires routine checkups just like your medical health does. On the upside though, it's much more acceptable to complete THIS one while in your pajamas and with a side of coffee and chocolate cake.

In case you've never stopped to think of it this way – you have permission to do what is right for YOUR household, regardless of whether it's right for anyone else's or it's what anyone else thinks you "should" be doing, and regardless of whether it's what society's messages are all telling you to do! You do not need to keep up with any person or trend or societal "norm". You and your home do not need to look a certain way or function a certain way to please anyone who doesn't live there. This is YOUR life; these are YOUR home, money, journey, and goals that we're talking about. No one else's. Stop and intentionally think about what is important to you, now and for the future. Don't let a fleeting desire to appease anyone else derail your focus and progress on the future goals you have in mind for you and your family.

Let's be real here – there are people whose actual job is to try to convince you that you "need" a particular item or lifestyle. Whether they're being paid by the product companies, the advertisers, or for "clicks," their content revolves around convincing you that spending money on a certain item will keep you or your home in style, magically solve your problems (even if you didn't know you had them), make your life easier, or make you a better and happier mom/homemaker/woman in general. Am I suggesting that everything they're promoting is worthless? Of course not. I love some fabulous Amazon finds and newly discovered kitchen gadgets as much as anyone! (And if anyone ever invents jeans that truly give me my pre-babies figure back, but also fit like old comfy sweatpants? Just take all my money.) I'm not saying you should never buy the products (though obviously you shouldn't if you can't afford to) – I'm saying you shouldn't buy into the image. Buying into the *image* is what entices you to buy products you don't actually need, won't truly use, or just plain shouldn't be spending money on.

Learn to realistically assess whether an expenditure is a need or simply a want. While you may read that and think "well, duh", most of us don't stop to think about how much money we're truly spending each month on items that aren't an *actual* necessity, especially when it's little things here and there. (There's a reason it's termed "the latte factor.") Unfortunately, the little things add up in a bad way here just the same way as they add up in a good way when we were discussing quick cleaning habits. Am I about to tell you to cut out everything that's not an absolute necessity in your budget? No (unless you're currently in a financial situation where that IS needed). Forcing yourself to add up how much you spend on non-necessities each month though can be extremely eye-opening. Many of us can spend a lot more on small, mindless purchases in a month than we realize. If you don't track and categorize your spending, you'll never truly know where your money is going and won't understand why you don't have more to show for all the hard work you do. Smart phones, streaming subscriptions, take-out/drive-thru food, beauty/hair appointments, coffees/teas to go…none of those are truly necessary. (Tough love again, I know – but stick with it.) Again, am I suggesting that you cancel your cell phone and your Netflix subscription? No. If you're currently in a dire financial situation and are having trouble paying for your actual needs – adequate (not fancy) living quarters, food for your family, electricity and running water, etc. – then by all means, please get rid of every non-essential expenditure that you can so that you can get back on your feet. Chances are though, if you're reading this then you don't feel like your financial circumstances are quite that serious, but you'd still enjoy the prospect of some extra "wiggle room" in your monthly budget. Regardless of your current financial situation, you can benefit from sitting down and taking a good, hard look at where each of your dollars has been going. You may be surprised to find that there's more "fluff" that you could cut out than you thought!

Don't get me wrong, I'm in favor of "treating" yourself occasionally (within reason). But if you do it on a daily basis, is it really a "treat" or is it just a frivolous over-spending habit that you've been justifying to yourself? An amazing question I once heard was "do you want to *feel* rich or *be* rich?" You'll never reach the second one if you're continually over-indulging the first one. Living above your means will only give you temporary satisfaction (if that) and will ultimately cause you added stress both short-term (when you get the bill or realize next week that you now have less money for groceries) and farther down the road (because you've consistently saved less and spent more and now have less to show for your efforts/work than you could have).

If you recognize that you have some overspending habits that you want to change but this area is hard for you, try this – treat your finances like you're being PAID to manage them! I'm serious. Approach your budget and every expenditure that you make like it's literally your job. If you worked for an amazing company with a fabulous boss that you adored, and you were in charge of the company's budget, would you want to have to go tell your boss every week that you piddled away large chunks of the company's money on unneeded expenditures that weren't in the budget, and you have very little to show for it?? Absolutely not. So why continue doing this to yourself?! That amazing boss that you really want to impress? She represents Future You. The sooner that you get control of your budget and finances so that you can start making your money work *for* you as best as possible, the more Future You is going to love you for it. [Bonus: the longer that you model responsible spending habits and having affirmative control over your finances to your children, the better you set them up for success once they're adults too.] Learn how to say "no" to yourself. Parent yourself if necessary! Heck, do it out loud where your kids can hear you – if they're going to witness mom talking to herself, at least it'll be something constructive that they can learn from, right?

In the last chapter on routines, we talked about writing them down and having them easily visible as a reminder of your goal.

The same concept can work with budgeting too! There's a *reason* you're wanting to get better control of your budget. Maybe you're trying to save up for a car or house; maybe you're tired of living week by week, paycheck to paycheck; maybe you're just tired of wanting to cry every time you check out at the grocery store; maybe you have debt you want to pay off; maybe you're realizing how quickly the years go by and that you'll have a kid going to college before you know it. Whatever your reason(s) for wanting to improve this part of your life, *that's* what you need to keep in front of you. Take a picture of something that obviously and easily represents your "why" (such as a pic of somewhere you want to go with your family or a graph of paying off your mortgage) and make that the background and wallpaper on your phone. This way, anytime you're out shopping and are tempted to make an impulse purchase, chances are that at some point before you check out, you'll look at your phone – and then you'll be reminded why you should put that item back. Take it a step further and print out a copy to tape to your wallet – now you literally can't pull out your card to swipe without seeing the reminder! If online shopping is your weakness (anyone else need to join the founding chapter of Amazon Anonymous?), then take a few minutes and go delete your payment information from any apps you use. It may seem like a small, inconsequential thing, but the added convenience of already having your payment information saved to where you only have to click "buy now" is what's encouraging you to mindlessly shop. Now if you try to make an online purchase, you'll still be forced to look at your "why" reminder when you go to get your card from your wallet. Also, research shows that the retail therapy "high" that we get while online shopping goes away once you finish making your purchase. That means the temporary endorphin hit that you got is already gone *before your item is even delivered to you*! So, you and your bank account will both be better off if you just enjoy browsing online and even adding items to your cart – but don't actually purchase them. Chances are that the next time you look at that online cart in a few days you'll realize that you don't actually need (or even want) that item anymore and you can delete it – without having depleted some of your precious bank funds in the process.

Like we discussed above, it's hard to figure out where you can save money or "tighten your belt" if you don't realistically know where all your money has been going. So, if you haven't done this before, the easiest place to start is to print out all your transactions from the last 60 days (including your checking account, savings account, and all credit cards or store cards). Then grab a few different colors of pens or highlighters, decide on a color for each category (house bills, groceries, eating out, medical, etc.) and start color-coding. Once you're done, go through and add up one color at a time and write down your totals for each 30-day period. Is it a bit tedious? Yes. Is it necessary to be able to see where you've actually been spending all your money? Also yes. [I know there are apps that can help you do this, and if you want to use one from here on out then great. But I urge you to do this the first time on paper, because it truly makes a bigger impact on your brain if you have to physically mark/highlight things yourself and then write out the category totals by hand.] Once you've completed this and gotten over your own personal "sticker shock," you'll have a clearer understanding of what items in your budget are fairly static (there's not much you can do about your mortgage total each month) and how much you need to budget for those, versus which ones are more flexible (such as eating out, shopping and groceries) and therefore offer the best chance of being able to help you lower your monthly expenditures.

If you've never tried to have a household budget, there are scores of opinions out there for how to do it. We're going for simplicity though, right? So, let's just try the two simplest ways. One is what you probably automatically think of as a "budget," which is basically to just declare how much you're going to aim to spend on each category for the month. I call this the "goal-based budget." It works fine for some people, so if you try this and feel like it's effective then there you go! For some people though, they find it hard to keep themselves on track this way or find it too easy to go over-budget because there's money coming in that wasn't really accounted for in the category goals. If you're in the second group, consider trying a "zero-based budget." A quick online search will provide you with plenty of resources with more details on how to make this work for you, but in a nutshell you're "spending" all of your money for the month before it comes in. Don't get too excited (or panicked) – this does NOT mean you're literally spending money that you don't even have yet (that's definitely not the way to reach any financial goals). It simply means that you take the amount of money you expect to have come in for the month and decide beforehand where every single dollar is going – all the way until you have zero. Again, you're not *actually* spending all of it! You're allocating all of it (to bills, savings, groceries, a Christmas fund, shopping money, etc.) so that you know exactly how every penny you make should be getting used. This prevents any "free-floating" money from getting spent on frivolous items or mindless shopping when it could have been added to your savings account or helped pay off more debt.

The "default" when discussing budgeting is usually to discuss your spending per month. Remember though, this is supposed to be about finding what works for *you* and makes the most sense in your life. While I do still suggest you track things on a monthly basis (since there are certain bills that are only a factor once a month), depending on how and when the people in your household get paid it may make more sense to handle your budget on a weekly basis. Keeping in mind when you get paid and when certain bills are due can help avoid problems like spending too much at the grocery store the same week that you're having to pay your mortgage and your utility bills. Instead, you can be proactive and plan on purchasing a smaller amount of groceries that week, knowing that you'll be giving yourself a larger grocery amount the next week – AND saving yourself the stress of having your funds be a little too tight in between those paychecks because you didn't proactively plan.

Regardless of what budgeting method you choose, it can be frustrating and stressful to get to the end of a month and realize that you went over-budget in some areas without even realizing it. My favorite easy way to try to prevent this is to keep a list either on paper (that you always have with you) or on your phone. At the beginning of the month, make a section for each category and write down the budget you have for it. If it's easier for you to handle breaking things down by week (especially for groceries), do it that way. Then, every time you spend ANY money, write it down under the category it was for and subtract it from your budget, then write down your *new* remaining budget total for that category. I promise, this takes less than a minute to do whenever you make a purchase. It's totally worth it too, because now at any given moment you have an updated amount showing you how much you have left in your budget for the month/week in that category.

Seeing the running total in black and white every time you spend money is much more effective at keeping you on track than just roughly guessing at the totals in your head. It helps save you from inevitably realizing at the end of the month that you were off in your estimations – often because you weren't factoring in the smaller expenditures (like "just grabbing a few more things at the store" and "just grabbing a quick meal while we're out") which all add up more than we realize.

Okay, we're on the home stretch – I promise! Just a little more (with some random tips for saving money on non-grocery bills) and then we'll switch gears in the next chapter to stuff that's much more fun!

Although there's not much you can do (short of very drastic changes) to adjust your housing cost each month (mortgage or rent), there are some ways to save on the rest of your household bills. For instance, set a reminder on your phone calendar or planner for the month before your insurance (car, home, etc.) renews each year to shop around for quotes to save money. If you pull up the declaration page (the summary page) of your current insurance, getting other quotes should be fairly painless because you can ask them to just use the same coverage as what you currently have for comparison. If you do find something cheaper, talk to your current company about what you found first and see if they can match it – then you've saved money AND didn't have to handle any paperwork to switch policies! You can do the same thing for cell phone bills, internet service, etc.

In some areas, you can do the same thing for your utility bills. Even if you don't have that option though, there are other ways you can lower your utility costs. Try using a timer for showers to save on your water bill (plus it's more eco-friendly). Shortening daily showers by 5 minutes will reduce your water usage by thousands of gallons each year. Plus, if you're a morning showerer it'll give you back 5 minutes in your morning schedule! Consider hanging most of your clothes to dry, rather than using your dryer (which can contribute a lot to your utility costs). If it's winter and your home heating costs are destroying your budget, lower your thermostat a few degrees and have everyone in the home bundle up or layer their clothes. Open your window blinds during the day to let the sun in to help heat the house! If it's summer and the cost of cooling your home is getting insane, look for similar ways that you can reduce your energy usage by avoiding activities that heat up your home (since there's a limit to how many layers of clothes you can take off if you're hot). Keep your blinds and curtains closed to keep OUT the sun (unlike in the winter) so that it's not raising the ambient temperature in your home. As we talked about in the cooking section, try to avoid using your oven since it will heat up your kitchen and uses more electricity than a slow cooker or other small appliance. Tips like these may sound like common sense to you, or they may sound drastic because they impede some of the conveniences that you're used to – but either way, getting creative around the house is one of the best ways to help lower costs when you're in a super tight spot money-wise.

'Tis the Season (for Budgeting):

The last set of budgeting tips that follow is more about special occasions and holidays, rather than your everyday activities. The reason they're included though is because occasions like

Christmas, birthdays, etc. can too easily wreak havoc on your finances if you let them. Even when we have the best of intentions, we often make purchases for these occasions out of habit rather than stopping to think about how we could do things differently and save ourselves from unnecessary spending and stress.

You may not have control over when loved ones decide to get married, but that doesn't happen very often. The rest of the holidays, birthdays, and other special occasions, on the other hand, come every year and always at the same time – so there's no surprise, and no reason to not prepare beforehand! While many of these tips are given using Christmas as an example, they apply to any holiday, birthday or other special occasion that may come up. None of them are made any more special by stressing yourself out or putting yourself into debt and avoiding these will end up letting you actually enjoy the occasions even more. As you've figured out by now, a lot of the tips in this book focus on ways that proactive planning and prepping beforehand can save you stress (and money). The holidays are no different!

Let's start with some tips that will help before you even buy the first gift.

Want to be able to ADD money to your holiday budget (for Christmas for instance)? You know the holiday is coming (again, same time every year, folks!), so why not try to tighten your purse strings in other categories beforehand so that you can save that money for more holiday fun? For instance, if your regular monthly budget includes $200 a month spent on take-out or going out to eat, then why not cut that in half for a month or two before the holidays so that you can use it for Christmas spending instead? Don't just *say* that's what you did though, especially if you're still working on your budgeting/spending habits. Instead, actually pull out the cash that you're going to allocate in this way and put it away to use for your Christmas shopping, and make sure you write it down as part of the money you "spent" in October (or whatever month). This will keep you from trying to spend the same money twice if you didn't *actually* end up curbing your eat-out spending the month before. (If you look back at the end of the month and realize you didn't actually cut that spending in half, then no cheating – go put the cash back into your account so that you don't throw off your budget.) If this sounds like an idea you'd like, why not try doing it for every month next year – can you imagine how amazing it would feel to bankroll all of your holiday spending next year without ever having to change your normal monthly budget and without putting anything on credit cards??

Regardless of what specific holidays you celebrate, many people spend a LOT of money near the end of the year on purchasing gifts. Parents of young kids often spend even more, depending on whether Santa visits their house and what he tends to bring (wink, wink). So, what can you do to help curb the financial stress for that time of year while still being able to fully enjoy it?

First, let's start with whether the money you'd be spending will actually result in the outcome that you truly want. Approach gift-giving as a way of showing your gratitude and how thankful you are to have this person in your life. You're presenting a gift to this person to make them feel loved. That's truly the purpose of the gift, right? So, why then do we let ourselves get told by advertisers and media that we have to buy certain things or spend a certain amount in order to show our love and appreciation? "It's the thought that counts" isn't just a cliché. It's a reminder that the entire purpose behind gift-giving is to let the recipient know that you were thinking of them. It doesn't have to take a ton of money to do this! Chances are, even if you haven't read The Five Love Languages, you've at least heard of the concept. The reason I bring that up is this – why put yourself into debt and stress yourself out trying to find the "perfect" gift for everyone when many of the people you're buying for don't have "receiving gifts" as their love language?

Critically look at your gift list. Do you really have to *buy* something for everyone on the list? That person on your list who's so hard to buy for because they "have everything?" What if they really DO have everything that they need? Why not bake or make something for them instead? (You can get your kids involved too!) A consumable gift still shows the person that you care and wanted to acknowledge them, AND it doesn't burden them with receiving something they may not truly need or have space for in their home. (If you love them, why would you want to add to their guilt clutter??) Why incur debt and stress trying to choose something that they probably don't really need, when something less expensive and consumable (such as homemade food or drinks) can show them your love just as well? It may arguably be an even *better* representation of your affection since it shows that you not only thought about including them, but also acknowledges that they are worth you spending some of your precious time on to put something together for them (which is also more personable than just checking their name off a list when you grabbed something in Target). Speaking of time, also think about gifts that involve time together or require time to set up. Which would that grandma prefer – new family photos with all her family together, or that random item you were considering at the store?

Reevaluate your holiday habits. No matter what the tradition is, I promise that it's not worth jeopardizing your ability to pay your bills next month and I can assure you that no one who loves you would want you to put yourself in that position either. Maybe suggest to your family that you start a Sneaky Santa gift exchange instead of buying for everyone or consider drawing names to exchange gifts. Perhaps even get everyone on board to agree to not buy ANY gifts for each other this year, or to only gift things that you made yourself, or only buy for the young kids, etc. – whatever helps reduce the financial stress for everyone in the family. We've done different variations of this in my own family. One year we drew names and set a rule that you had to make the gift yourself. Another year we drew names, set a specific dollar amount, and declared that each gift *had* to be a gift card/certificate – but it couldn't be to a large retailer or "big box" store (only local shops or services were allowed). Yet another year, we chose to not give gifts to each other but to instead adopt a local family. We got information on the ages and interests of the family members and anything they particularly needed, and then each person in our family contributed what they were able to or took responsibility for certain parts of the list we came up with. Gifts were wrapped and labeled and delivered to the family on Christmas Eve. On Christmas Day, our family gathered together and ate, played board games, told stories, and focused solely on enjoying each other's company. It was one of the best Christmases ever!

If you *are* going to be purchasing gifts though, what can you do to try to not break the bank? First, start with that dreaded B-word: budget. Rather than starting off with a dollar amount in mind that you're going to spend on each person on your list, do it the other way around – decide what you can realistically afford to spend in *total* for the occasion. Then make a list of every person and every single *thing* that you intend to spend money on. Don't forget to add in items such as ingredients needed for any extra baking/cooking that you do, gifts for teachers/classmates/coworkers, items you may gift to neighbors, etc. Include special activities that you want to do (such as attending a light show or festival or going to a special holiday event) and the costs associated with those as well. NOW, once you have a full picture of EVERYTHING that will require funds during this holiday, you can subtract the costs for things like activities and baking from your total budget and then divide what's *left* among the people that you want to buy gifts for. Write a dollar amount next to each person/activity on your list and *stick to it*! This way you won't go over-budget and into debt by spending more than you realized or thought that you would. Approaching a holiday budget this way may not seem that different at first glance, but it helps you avoid the problems that come with not taking smaller expenditures into account or not realizing how much you're really spending. Don't be the person who says "we're only going to spend $1,000 total on Christmas this year" …and then realizes in January that you *actually* spent closer to $2,000.

Treat the budget list you made just like one of your regular budget categories. If you wrote that your budget allows you to spend $40 on John for Christmas, then once you buy something for John *write it down* and either cross him off the list (if you spent the full $40) or adjust how much you have left to spend on him (if you spent less than $40). Not only does it help you remember what you've already purchased for each person, but it also makes you stay on track budget-wise so that you won't unintentionally overspend. Also, keep in mind the *spirit* of the budget limit. What do I mean by that? Well, let's say you find a great gift for John on Amazon. It's normally $40, but you're lucky enough to catch a lightning deal on it and snag it for $25. Does that automatically mean that you still "need" to spend another $15 on John? NO! If you're able to find deals on gifts, let the savings help you and your budget. You found a gift that is *valued* at $40 – do you think John cares that you didn't actually have to pay as much for it?! I say no. (If John says yes, maybe he just needs coal for Christmas!) Again, it's about the spirit and intent of the gift-giving – not how many dollars you actually had to spend on it.

Another way to help ease the strain on your wallet when it comes to gifts (especially for kids) is to make a "gift closet." Whenever stores have toys, art kits, etc. on clearance, I try to grab a few that I know will work for the age ranges of kids that I'm typically buying for. (Did you know that Target has a massive toy clearance sale twice a year?) I put them away in my "gift closet" throughout the year, and then I always have a stash of gifts to pull from for birthday parties, Christmas, etc.! It may not seem like a big deal, but it saves you in a pinch if you find out last-minute about a birthday party invitation for one of your kids and it definitely helps save money throughout the year (and at Christmas) since all the items were purchased for deeply discounted prices. The "gift closet" doesn't have to involve an actual closet either – in some of our houses it was a shelf in our hall closet; sometimes it's been a tote bin under my bed; other times it's been a drawer or two in my dresser or a certain spot in the garage or attic. Just find something that works for you! Most importantly, remember to go "shop" from your gift closet before shopping at a store for a birthday or holiday gift. (Saving money by buying items on clearance doesn't do you much good if you forget to use them and still go pay full price for something else later!)

Last but not least, did you include wrapping supplies in your budget? If you have a particularly tight holiday budget, this is an item that can definitely make or break you. Consider spending less on wrapping supplies by buying simple, brown craft paper and then using pretty ribbon – or let your kids decorate the paper themselves! Perhaps make it a family activity one night to have them help you choose old photos of each recipient and then print out the pictures on paper to tape onto the packages in lieu of a name tag. It's all going to be torn up and tossed anyway, so find ways to make it cute without spending a ton of money that will *literally* get thrown away.

PART II:
The Icing on Top

Chapter 7: Five Minutes Counts

Think five minutes can't make much difference? Surely by now you know better! This chapter is short and sweet because it's all about how you can use just five minutes to "level up" in any area of your life. Numerous tips that we've discussed so far can be done quickly but have a big impact. Look at just a few examples that we've already talked about that can all be done in five minutes or less:

- 5-minute pick-ups around your house to tidy things quickly
- 5 minutes spent decluttering or organizing
- Having everyone spend 5 minutes on Sunday to choose their clothes for the week
- 5 minutes to take out meat to thaw and/or pull out other ingredients to have ready for the next night's dinner
- 5 minutes to listen to a podcast or watch a video on a topic that you want to advance in (personal financial planning, for example)
- 5 minutes to make an easy meal plan for the upcoming week
- 5 minutes to prep lunches for the next day
- 5 minutes on Sunday evening to plan and schedule your week
- 5 minutes to load and set the dishwasher before bed

- 5 minutes to throw in/switch laundry before bed or before you leave the house
- Less than 5 minutes to make your bed in the morning
- 5 minutes to unload the dishwasher in the morning (or have your kids do it in the morning or after school)
- 5 minutes to send that email or make that phone call that you've been putting off

And that's just a handful of them! Whether you realized it or not, you've probably thought of several other ideas while reading the previous chapters. Try focusing on areas/topics that we covered that you immediately thought "I don't have time for that," and see what you can come up with that would fit into that category but not take much time. For instance, do you often find yourself neglecting self-care because you "don't have time?" Brainstorm a list of quick self-care ideas that you can refer to when you feel especially stressed or drained. Do you enjoy putting on a facial mask or other pampering skincare, but rarely leave yourself time to do it before bed? Try putting one on while you bathe a younger child or while you clean the kitchen at night! Would you love to incorporate yoga into your day but can't fit a class into your schedule? Look online or on YouTube and find a few morning and evening poses that you can incorporate into your morning and evening routines. Does being outside in nature calm you? Then give yourself a few minutes to sit outside with some warm tea or go for a short walk (even if it's just around your backyard). Think about things that make you happy or calm your stress, and then figure out how to fit them into a short window of time whenever you have it (and if you're tempted to say you don't have it, then make it!) – listen to a favorite soothing song or two…meditate…stop right that minute and schedule an upcoming meetup with a friend. Even just five minutes spent doing something that feeds your soul is infinitely worth it!

What about other ways you can use a handful of minutes to help make life easier for Future You? Add a few extra minutes to the time you'll already be in the kitchen cooking and use it to make extra food to freeze for later. Standing at the stove browning meat for dinner? Then why not also mix up some muffin batter while you're standing there, and then let the muffins bake while you eat dinner. Bam – now you have muffins to freeze or use for breakfasts during the week! Like we discussed in the cooking/food chapters, it takes less than five minutes to make two pots of chili at the same time instead of just one, and then you have one to freeze for later. Chopping some fresh produce? Chop a little extra and bag it for your freezer or to save yourself time later in the week for another meal. Unloading groceries? Why not spend a few extra minutes to decant or transfer certain items into their bins/baskets right now? Then you can toss the box or bag into your recycling bin and not have to worry about that task later (or worry that you won't get to it and then won't realize until it's too late that you've run out of granola bars). If you have a tendency to have to throw away old leftovers or other items that have gone bad in your refrigerator, how about spending five minutes to quickly organize your fridge to help you better utilize (not lose) leftovers, partial items, etc.? Perhaps designate part of an eye-level shelf in the fridge for "use first" items and even label it or tape a sign to the edge of that shelf to help the whole family get in the habit of grabbing these items first!

Trying to get better control over your finances and implement better budgeting habits? Make it part of your evening routine to spend five minutes each night logging in any purchases and expenditures that day into your budget tracker and subtracting those from your weekly/monthly budget for each category.

Really wanting to be kind to Future You? How about helping her AND helping your kids by taking the five extra minutes to teach or show them how to do something for themselves? It helps them become more independent and self-assured, and it moves you that much closer to not always having to be the one to do it (whatever "it" is)!

The list of ways that we can utilize even just a few minutes is endless. So, the next time you find yourself thinking that you "only" have five minutes, switch gears and learn to start thinking instead about all you *can* do in those five minutes to help Future You's life be easier. Even if you can't finish something in five minutes (or however long you have), do however much you can anyway – you'll have gotten that much *more* done than if you hadn't bothered at all, and it'll be that much better when you're able to come back to it later. Am I saying you should always be go-go-go and never stop to just breathe or take a break for a few minutes? Absolutely NOT. However, the more you make it a habit to utilize little pockets of "only five minutes" effectively, the more you'll find that you've accomplished enough by the end of the day that you can take longer breaks and take more time for yourself without feeling any guilt.

Chapter 8: Simply Special
(Easy ways to make things memorable for your kids)

Ok, the irony is not lost on me – most of this book is focused on making things easier for you and pointing out that you don't need to be a "Perfect Pinterest Mom," and then you get to this chapter and it sounds like something you'd see on, well, Pinterest. I promise though, this chapter is still in line with the premise of everything else in here! If doing stuff like this does not interest you and/or seems way too "extra" for your tastes, that's cool – this is the one time I'll say it's okay to skip ahead! The reason I included this chapter though is because so many other moms have said that they would love to do little things to make occasions and certain days extra fun or special for their kids, but they just don't know what to do or where to start and trying to look through all those "pins" gets overwhelming.

So, that's where this chapter comes in – *simple* ways to make things just a little extra special. While the majority of the ideas and suggestions in this book are focused on helping you save time and/or money, this section is admittedly a little different. Don't worry though – while none of these ideas will actually *save* you time or money, they won't cost you much either. What they WILL do is help you feel like SuperMom to your kids (and they'll agree), with as little stress and effort as possible. There are plenty of free or cheap ways you can make things special. Kids are easier to please than we give them credit for, and it's generally the quality time and the memory that are the most special to them (not how much money was spent).

Some of these are just general ideas and tips that you can use as a jumping-off point for whatever you're celebrating and make it your own; others are occasion/season specific to help give you additional inspiration. Many of the ideas involve food, because let's face it – kids like to eat, a lot. They also get a kick out of anything that makes their food special or out of the ordinary (plus making fun tweaks to food is usually super cheap and easy). Let's start with the general ideas first, then we'll get into some suggestions for particular holidays.

Try taking a family activity that you already do and giving it a fun twist to "theme" it to whatever the occasion is. Perhaps you enjoy family game nights – then try out a new game that fits with what you're celebrating and have fitting themed snacks. If you're celebrating the end of the school year and the start of summer, try some fun DIY backyard carnival-style games or let the kids make homemade ice cream in a bag! Another easy way to kick up the celebration factor a notch is to use special plates and cups that day; they can be special family heirloom ones or decorative themed paper goods from the dollar store. It may seem like a meaningless detail to you, but it's sure to excite young kids (nothing says "fun time" like fun paper party plates)! You can even take this tip a step further and have one very special plate that each person gets to use when it's their birthday or they're the person being celebrated (for whatever reason) that day.

While it's easy for kids to feel special on their birthday (since the day is literally being celebrated because they were born), what about easy ways to make different holidays feel more festive and fun (without breaking your bank)? As mentioned above, one of the easiest ways is with food. Just a few extra seconds to add in a little color or add something on top, and presto – instant celebratory fun food! Whipped cream doesn't have lots of sugar and makes food seem extra special for kids. Whipped cream + sprinkles = celebration (in a kid's eyes)! (Don't believe me? Try adding whipped cream or sprinkle on top of basically anything and see what reaction you get.) A plain jello cup is just jello, but a green jello cup with whip cream and sprinkles on top is Grinch jello! Red jello with whip cream and sprinkles (or red mini chips) is a special Valentine's Day treat. You get the idea! Keep items like sprinkles, whipped cream, food coloring, seasonal fruit, and colored vanilla mini chips on hand at all times and you're always prepared to turn a regular meal or snack/treat into something festive at the drop of a hat! Want a few specific ideas to start with? Try these:

- Make any day during the Christmas season extra festive with a special Christmas breakfast –
    - Green food coloring kicks pancakes or waffles up a notch and can transform them into Grinch pancakes, Christmas tree waffles (just cut them

into triangles), etc. Use it to dye the icing for cinnamon rolls or even scrambled eggs too!

- o Let the kids make a "gingerbread" house for breakfast out of waffles, toast or even Pop-Tarts! Whipped cream makes great "mortar" without adding the sugar of actual icing. A waffle "gingerbread" house using whipped cream and strawberries is not only festive and fun to make, but it's even healthier than regular waffles with syrup.
- o My kids love having a snowman breakfast during Christmas break – white powdered donut "snowmen" with mini chocolate chip faces and matching snowmen made with cinnamon rolls. The simple "cherry" on top? Milk in clear plastic cups that I draw snowmen faces on with a Sharpie. Fancy? No. Do the kids love it? Absolutely.

- Take seasonal snacks up a notch too –
  - o Green food coloring and melted marshmallows can give you "Grinch popcorn" or green Rice Krispie treats (that can also be cut with cookie cutters into Christmas trees or clover shapes for St. Patrick's Day).
  - o Grab some ingredients at the dollar store to make cookies and let the kids decorate them as an afternoon activity.

- Snag some craft supplies at the dollar store and let the kids entertain themselves while they create a holiday craft. Is it Christmas time? Get a cheap t-shirt and let them create ugly Christmas "sweaters" (plus you'll get a cute pic out of it)!
- Have the kids help you brainstorm ideas for ways to give back – try a Random Acts of Kindness countdown to do as a family during the holidays, or let them help you shop for gifts that will be donated for an Angel tree or Operation Christmas Child or another charity of your choice.
- Make a list together of free activities to do as a family during the holiday season, such as walking or driving around to view neighborhood Christmas lights or going to free community events and festivals.
- Have family movie nights – watch a movie that fits the season/occasion and let the kids help make themed snacks beforehand. Did they already make ugly Christmas "sweater" shirts? Have everyone wear those for movie night too!
- Celebrating Easter? Make things simple for yourself (and the kids) by using color-coordinated plastic eggs (1 color for each kid) for egg hunts – it helps ensure that each kid gets their fair share of the eggs, plus it makes it easier to know for sure if there are any still not-found! You can also have a "wild color" that's up for grabs by anyone.

- Have an Easter egg hunt lunch (this has always been one of my kids' favorites)! Instead of candy, fill the eggs with lunch items (bite size cubes of turkey, cheese, grapes, pretzel sticks, raisins, etc.) and then go hide them right before lunchtime. The kids will have fun hunting for all the eggs and then they get to immediately sit down and eat their "goodies." This is one that can easily be done at home in your own yard or take it to go and bring everything to a park so they can play after eating as well!
- Make a family Thankful Pumpkin during the month of November to celebrate Thanksgiving. Buy a pumpkin (real or faux; you can often get them on sale the day after Halloween) and use a Sharpie to let each family member write something on the pumpkin that you're thankful for each day.

Often it takes little more than framing *how* you talk about a meal or activity to make it seem extra special for your kids. Tell them you're having special "Tell All Tacos" for dinner on the first day of school as a prompt for everyone to take turns telling about their day. Print out a fun "chalkboard" sign to set on the table when they have breakfast on the first and last days of school. Give a meal a special name, use some fun napkins or plates, or even print a little sign to set on the table and you've instantly elevated a regular meal into something special. While spending a few extra minutes on different colored food, party plates/napkins/signs or using cute holiday-themed names may seem insignificant to you, these are the kinds of fun details that turn an otherwise normal day or activity into a festive, memorable event that your kids will look forward to and fondly reminisce on for years to come – and it requires very little extra time or money to make it happen.

Chapter 9: Big or Small? More or Less? (Simple Decorating Tips)

Everyone has different tastes in everything from food to clothes to décor. So, this chapter is *not* about telling you to decorate your home with a certain style or in a certain way. It's your home – you do what makes YOU happy! What follows will just be some general tips and simple ideas to help you if you're stuck on trying to get your home to have the "feel" that you want. Not only does this make you feel happier when you look around your home, but getting your spaces to where you're pleased with them even makes you more likely to maintain the effort required to keep them tidy and clean!

The best place to start with is the basic rule that less is more. It's often easy to look at a space and feel like it "needs something" because it doesn't have the look or feel that we want, and so we go grab some random knick-knacks at Target or Home Goods. But then it still doesn't "feel right," so we try more/new items. This can easily turn into a vicious cycle that only results in creating clutter, wasting your money, and frustrating you with your home! Instead, try doing the exact opposite of this. What room came to mind first when reading the last few sentences? Grab an empty box or tote and go to that room. Gather up all the knick-knacks, decorations, etc. (even wall décor, unless it's very large pieces) and put them in the box. Empty the room of everything except furniture and things that are absolutely necessary. Now, WAIT. Leave the room! Ideally, wait at least a day (maybe more); otherwise, wait at least an hour while you go do something in another part of your home. Once you come back, stop and really take in how the room feels this way. Now you can start to add some items back in, BUT don't just automatically go put everything back where it was. Start with either larger statement pieces or items that mean the most to you that you really want to have out to display. (If you're doing this to more than one room at once, stop and challenge yourself to consider placing items into a different room than where they were before – they'll feel new!) Try adding only a few large or important items in, and then stop again. Wait. See how the room feels now. Keep in mind that having lots of small items in a space creates lots of visual clutter, which can unknowingly create stress or anxiety when you come into the room. If there are small items that you truly want to display, group them together rather than spreading them all out. Your eyes need places around the room to "rest", where they are free from visual stimulation.

Try spreading this process out over at least a week, or even two. Give yourself a day or two each time that you've added something(s) to live with it and see it fresh several times (after you've been out of the house for a bit) before you consider adding in more items. Once you notice that you feel happier with the space, *leave it alone* for now. If it's the items themselves that you're not happy with or that you don't like, don't put them back just because you have them. See if there are pieces around your home that you can move to other rooms instead (shop your own stuff!), or else leave the space alone for now and really put thought into where you still feel like you need "something", what kind of "something" you might want there – and then be intentional about not buying an item to fill the space until you find exactly what you had in mind and feels right. It's better to have the room be a little barer than you're used to than to have it remain cluttered and filled with items that don't make you happy or serve you.

As mentioned above, small items can be problematic because they can easily turn into "visual clutter" (even if they're items you want to keep and you don't think of them as "clutter"). If you have certain sentimental items that are special to you, consider displaying them rather than keeping them hidden away in a box or tote somewhere. Let them be where you can enjoy and appreciate them – they may even spark some neat conversations with friends when they come over! If they mostly consist of smaller items though, then rather than spreading them out throughout a room or your entire home, group them together (you can make a few groups if you're working with a large collection). This will give these items that you love more of an impact and will let your eyes recognize them together as one collection rather than lots of individual loose "clutter" items. This also helps your collection make a statement. It's your house and your items – let it make a statement that you love XYZ, not make a statement that your house is cluttered!

What about color? This is an area that's definitely determined by your personal tastes. Do you prefer soft neutral colors? Great! Are rich jewel tones what makes you happy? Awesome! Whatever color pallet you choose, just be smart with it. A safe plan is to use neutral colors for large items (such as couches) and then add pops of color with accent pieces. This makes it easy to change your style later on for little money. Paint is another great way to make a big difference for little money! I'm not just talking about painting your walls, either – don't forget about furniture. Find a piece with a good shape or features that you like and then transform it with paint. Chalk paint or other bonding paint is great for this because it doesn't require as much prep work. Try dollar stores or discount stores for wall art – you can always use some cheap craft paint to change the frame color or add an accent color to the art!

You can also easily add pops of color, along with texture, using textiles (i.e., fabric items). When used correctly, throw pillows, blankets and rugs can help pull together a room and give it the vibe you're after. If you like to change out pillows for different seasons or holidays (or just to have a change), try getting pillow covers so that you can just switch out the cover instead of the entire pillow – this makes it so much easier to store the ones you're not currently using (plus it's generally less expensive). Want to give your bedding an update? If all new bedding isn't in your budget, try just replacing your pillowcases! You can buy new pillowcases on Amazon for under $10 in many cases. This is a great tip to use for kids' bedrooms too since they outgrow styles/characters fairly often. Also, don't forget about rugs. While they're not as cheap as pillow covers or blankets (though you can find great rug deals on Amazon sometimes), rugs can be essential to tying your room together and giving it a cohesive, grounded feel. Last (for color) but not least, consider changing your light bulbs. Wondering what that has to do with color? Simply switching out fluorescent or "warm" tone lights for daylight LED bulbs (which are "cool") can completely change the look of the colors in your home. That's definitely simpler and faster than repainting your walls!

The last tip for decorating your home is to pay attention to height and weight (and I don't mean yours). Have you ever tried to decorate a bookshelf or mantle, and nothing you tried seemed quite right? A lot of times this is due to an imbalance in the height or "weight" of your items. Let's tackle weight first. By weight, I don't mean how heavy the item actually is, but more it's "visual" weight. Try this – visualize two large balls that are the exact same size, but one is a woven wicker ball and one is solid metal. Which one *looks* heavier and more solid? The metal ball, of course. Regardless of its actual weight, it carries more visual weight and will visually *feel* heavier on a shelf. This is important because the visual weight of an item matters just as much as it's actual physical size. If you put two groups of similar-size items on each end of a mantle and one group consists of items with more *visual* weight, then the display will never look "right." Mix the items up and try to keep a balance of visual weight so that no one part of a shelf or section of a room feels heavier and weighed down by its items more than the rest of the area.

Do you have to always maintain perfect symmetry and make everything on the shelf the same height and weight? Definitely not – in fact, doing so will often take away from the visual interest in that area. While balancing visual weight is important, when it comes to the *height* of your items, you'll want more variation. Not only do you want some variation in the height of the items on a shelf or mantle, but more importantly you also want to create height variations around the room. Stand in the middle of the room and slowly turn in a circle, looking at all the major items in the room. As your eye moves from your couch to a side table, to a table lamp, to art on the wall, to items on a mantle, to a floor lamp, to the love seat…you should notice your eyes moving up and down across varying heights around the room. If you don't, try rearranging some pieces and see if that helps the room flow better and feel more interesting.

The most important rule when it comes to decorating your home? Go with what YOU love, not what's "in." The current design trends will change just like fashion fads do and trying to constantly change up your home can get a lot more expensive than clothes. Your house should be a reflection of you and your family and should make *you* feel happy, peaceful and at home. What it does or doesn't do for anyone else is irrelevant. Home décor is just like everything else we've covered in this book – it's your life, so you find what works for you and makes you happier.

Chapter 10: Help Them Help You – Simple Parenting Hacks

Just like the budgeting chapter, let me be crystal clear here – I am NOT a parenting expert! I'm *absolutely* not a perfect parent (and I don't think one exists), but there are a few ideas and "hacks" that have worked with children I know (including my own) and made life in our homes run smoother. Nothing in this chapter involves discipline or general parenting philosophies; it's all about ways to make things easier for you and your kids so that they can learn to be independent, functioning members of the family while also helping you want to scream and pull your hair out less.

While it's probably a universal statement that we all want our kids to grow up to be capable, independent, functioning adults…it's surprisingly easy sometimes to forget the correlation that this means we need to help teach them how to get there. Do you want to still be doing all their laundry, cooking their food, cleaning their dishes, and generally picking up after them for the next forty years? Assuming that the answer is no, then consider this statement: you'll never get promoted if you don't train someone to replace you. In other words, unless your answer to the previous question was "yes," then you better train them how to do those things for themselves!

If your kids are old enough to walk, then they're old enough to start learning to help around the house. Starting with teaching them to pick up toys often makes sense, but too often parents basically stop there and only teach their kids to help with the kids' personal items. Young kids can help with all sorts of things! Even little ones can help put clothes into the washing machine or dryer, help pick up items off the floor, help wipe crumbs off the table, etc. Let them help you unload the silverware and any plastic plates/bowls/cups.

While we're talking about helping in your kitchen, why not consider moving certain items in order to let the kids learn to be more self-sufficient? For example, why not keep their plastic cups in a lower cabinet or drawer so that they can easily get their own cup for a drink or plate for a meal/snack – and also be able to easily help unload their clean dishes from the dishwasher! Instead of fretting over them putting the clean forks in the wrong spot, let them help and calmly "fix" anything that bothers you later (not right in front of them where it will discourage their innate love of helping). Yes, sometimes this can make the task feel like it takes a bit longer (than if you were doing it all yourself) but it's a process that is worth it for the future payoff. Not only are they learning how to participate in maintaining their home (while they're young enough to get excited about helping), but it also can help them develop more respect for the family home and their possessions since they get to witness firsthand the work that goes into having to clean up a mess that was made or even just maintain things.

Consider getting kid-sized cleaning aids such as brooms (try a handheld one with a dustpan) and vacuums (such as a rechargeable handheld one) and let them clean with you. While Mommy vacuums the carpet, little Jared can vacuum the couch or under the dining table. Give them a damp antibacterial microfiber cloth and let them go to town on wiping surfaces and dusting. Resist the urge to fret too much over them not doing things "correctly" or putting items in exactly the right place. The more you let them help with chores around the house, the more teachable moments you'll have so that you can gradually help them learn the correct placement of things, etc.

Teaching them how to do household chores when they're young is SO much easier than waiting until they're teenagers and trying to start then! Spending the extra time now to teach them how to do it while they're young will serve you (and them) better in the long run than spending the time to always do it yourself. The older your kids are when you start implementing household chores and responsibilities, the more likely that they're going to grumble and resist – and let's be honest, you're probably still going to have to show/teach them how you want it done almost as many times as if they were younger. So just go ahead and start when they're young! If that ship has already sailed and you missed the chance to start teaching these things early on though, don't let that discourage you and keep you from starting now. It is never too late! There are so many reasons why it is healthy and beneficial for them to learn what goes into keeping a house well-maintained, clean, and functional while they're still living at home.

I'm not suggesting that you treat your kids like a modern-day Cinderella. They shouldn't be responsible for *everything* around your house (you are the adult after all) – but chances are they're capable of handling more than they currently do. Trying to figure out the right balance on how many household chores to give your kids? One place to start is one chore per each year of their age (i.e., a 4-year-old has 4 chores, and a 7-year-old has 7). Yes, make sure the designated chores are age appropriate. Hard truth time though: if your kids can use an iPad, phone, or tablet, they can learn to operate the washing machine, dryer, dishwasher, etc. Again, I'm not saying you should send your 5-year-old to run the major appliances unsupervised – but start showing them how to now, and in a few years you'll "magically" have less laundry, etc. that you're responsible for!

Depending on the age of your kids and the level to which they've had household responsibilities (or not) up to this point, getting some resistance and grumbling from them can be expected (especially if they're older). Stay consistent though, and it will pay off for the entire family. After all, one of your main parenting goals is to raise them into self-sufficient adults, right? Find creative ways to avoid having to nag them about chores. Make it fun if you're all doing housework together – put on some music, dance and sing while you work, and set a timer to go off to mark that they've completed 10 minutes of cleaning (if that was the goal). If your home has an electronic device such as an Alexa or Echo, you can even tell it to set the reminders so that it will remind Ben each Tuesday at 4:30 that it's his laundry day. Young kids will love to "race against the clock" and try to beat the timer if you set it for 5 minutes to pick up toys. If some extra incentive is needed to help maintain the consistency needed to fully establish these new habits, you can also consider tying in a reward of something they enjoy doing with finishing the chore (such as they get 10 minutes of screen time once they've unloaded the dishwasher and cleaned their bathroom counters).

Just remember – kids watch and notice EVERYTHING, and they pick up on a lot more than we tend to give them credit for (especially our moods and attitudes). Be intentional about minding your attitude toward household chores and maintenance and try to project a spirit of thankfulness and happiness when doing them. Not only will this make a big difference in your children wanting to help participate, but it also helps them develop a spirit of gratitude for the home and surroundings that they've been given, which will serve them well for their entire lives. (Added bonus: it won't hurt you either to focus on keeping a positive attitude while you maintain your home.)

Lists work just as well for kids as they do for us. Make lists for your kids for things such as chores, daily morning routine, daily after-school tasks, and evening routine. For young children who can't read yet, simply use pictures! Even a toddler can look at a row of pictures and easily learn that pictures of a bathtub, a toothbrush, a book, and a bed mean that we take a bath, then brush our teeth, then have story time before bed. While the list itself may seem kind of pointless when they're that little (since you're obviously helping them to do all those activities anyway), helping them develop these habits early on will make the transition to having them be solely responsible for tasks themselves that much easier later! Your household's daily schedule and your general parenting style can be as laidback as you want, but don't ignore the fact that kids do well with clear, set expectations.

Want to teach them responsibility but still be more flexible? Try using chore cards/sticks rather than chore charts or lists. Simply write one chore/task on each index card (or popsicle stick, or tongue depressor, or whatever you want to use) and keep them all in a container. Each day/week/whatever each child can draw a card/stick and that's the chore they're responsible for that day. Keep completed ones separated out until all have been done and then place them all back in to start over. This helps with monotony for kids who would do better with variety than a set routine. (Bonus: it also cuts down on sibling bickering about "he/she always gets to do that one and I always have to do this one!") This system also allows the chore sticks/cards to double as consequences for undesirable behavior if you so choose. If you have a wider age range of kids, try having two sets and dividing the tasks in each so that they're more age appropriate. Don't want to do cards, sticks, or charts? Try dividing your house into zones/areas and assign each person a zone ("zone defense" if you will, for those sports mamas). Have a visible master list of what tasks need to be done for each zone, and then rotate who's responsible for each area every few weeks/months.

Lead by example! Just like we discussed earlier in the book that cleaning and tidying aren't the same thing, help your kids learn the value of having tidy habits and show them how much faster and easier it is to *clean* a home that's already tidy. Teach them to never leave a room without picking up after themselves – if they're going to stop playing with something, put it away. If they're finished eating, clean up their place and dishes. If they're done reading, put away the book. If they just finished showering, hang up their towel, deposit dirty clothes in the appropriate hamper, and make sure to wipe up any water that's dripped onto the floor or counters. Don't overwhelm them by trying to focus on too many things at once though. Just lead by example; talk to them about why you do things like this and work on one or two habits at a time. Before you know it, everyone in the family will have improved their household habits and you'll all enjoy a calmer, more stress-free home environment as a result.

To balance teaching kids the importance of taking care of what's theirs but also instilling the value of working to earn money, designate certain chores and household tasks as ones that are their responsibility as part of the household (that they do not get paid for). Choose other tasks (such as ones you usually do) as "extras" that they can choose to complete as well if they wish to earn money. In lieu of having a set "allowance" for our children, we offer chores and various home maintenance activities (such as seasonal tasks) that they can do to earn money if they choose. Basic responsibilities of living in the house and being part of the family are their required contribution without payment (putting away their things, keeping their rooms tidy, doing their laundry/dishes, etc.). Money can be earned by doing work that is not already part of their household contribution (such as extra yard work, washing windows, washing cars, etc.) and we make sure to have options available that are age appropriate for each kid.

Teaching your children about participating in the upkeep and maintenance of a home will benefit them for the rest of their lives. Want to know what can be even more invaluable? Helping them instill habits that will keep their home from ever getting unmanageable or overwhelming in the first place. As we discussed in the chapter in decluttering, kids can get overwhelmed by too much stuff even more easily than adults do – even (or especially) when it's their own toys! If you think this may be a problem in your house, consider decluttering their toys (and maybe take it a step further by separating what you do keep into groups to rotate through one group at a time). This doesn't have to be complicated or take long! Use a large basket or a tote for each group, sort the toys into the baskets/totes, and then keep only 1 out. Put the other(s) away somewhere that is easy enough for you to access, but where it's "out of sight, out of mind" for the kids. Then whenever you want to rotate toys, simply gather the ones that are out and put into their basket/tote, then go switch it out for one of the others. Simple! Let me clarify though – when I say to declutter their toys, I'm not saying to take on the task by yourself. It is not your responsibility to declutter your child's things. It IS your responsibility to teach them how to do it. It is a learned skill and behavior (which is why this book for you, an adult, spent so much time on it). It is also an important life skill. So regardless of their age, have them participate and go through the process with you (while keeping in mind that their age will of course affect their attention span), even if it means just doing it for spurts of 10 minutes at a time. Like many things, the teaching process can take time and patience – but just imagine the generational impact of helping your kids learn this NOW!

Similar to using pictures to help teach little ones about routines, they're also a great way to help kids learn to keep their things organized. Use pictures in their bedroom or playroom to show what goes in certain toy bins (blocks, dolls, puzzles, etc.) or which clothing items go in particular drawers. If they're just learning their letters/sounds, include the word with the picture – multiple teaching opportunities in one little label! While elementary age kids may not need to continue having labels/pictures on their clothes drawers, I still suggest keeping labels on toy bins – those items are the easiest ones to get mixed up. (If it doesn't bother you *or* your kids to have different categories of toys all mixed together and it doesn't seem to affect what they play with, feel free to skip categorizing toys. As always, you do what works for you!) Keep in mind though that if the kids continually have trouble with keeping toys picked up, it may be as simple as them just having too many. (*Hint – revisit the decluttering chapter!*)

If you don't feel that this is the case and think it's more of a discipline issue, try having a toy jail. Use an extra laundry hamper as the "toy jail" – anything not picked up properly at the end of the night goes into "jail" and is kept there for 24 hours (or a longer period if your kids are older) before it will be returned. Repeat offenders (the toys, not the kids) may have to go away for longer or be earned back. When our kids were a little younger, I also explained it this way: abandoned toys (those left out on the floor when they should have been put away) make me sad, just like abandoned animals do, and I want them to have a home. So, any toy found abandoned would be considered "homeless" and would be adopted out to a new home (meaning not ours)! Yes, the explanation was a little tongue-in-cheek, but it was effective. Of course, it's your home and your rules, so details as to how often and to what extent toys have to be picked up is up to your interpretation.

These last few parenting tips are more random, but equally useful. So, in no particular order, a few parting "hacks" –

1. If two kids are going to split something (like a cookie), let one cut and the other choose. I generally let the older sibling cut/split the item, and then the younger sibling gets to choose their "half." Not only does this reduce "his half is bigger" arguments, but it also gives them some gentle practice in conflict discussion and resolution.
2. Give kids win-win choices. A great example of this is for clothing – if they want some control over their outfits but you're not ready to give them free reign, frame it in a way that gives them the choice. "Do you want to wear the red shirt or the green shirt?" (Both of which *you* are fine with, but they're getting to make the final decision.)
3. Learn the phrase "different parents/houses have different rules" and use it often – it will come in handy more times during parenting than you'd guess, especially the older that your kids get!
4. Try having a "family pickup" each evening, where everyone works together for 5-10 minutes to reset each room in the house to what *should be* its default state. Kids are less likely to "revolt" if they see that everyone is pitching in, not just them.
5. Last but certainly not least – get them outside or get them in the tub! If outside isn't an option and a little one is having a "moment," try a bath. Water tends to calm and settle little ones almost as much as fresh air. Everyone will have a chance to hit their reset button, and you can

even check off wiping the counters and toilet while you're in there. If you can go outside though, do that. Time outside in nature is extremely beneficial for children for numerous reasons. It is for you as well, so go join them!

Chapter 11: Everything but the Kitchen Sink – Miscellaneous tips

We're on the home stretch, friends! Hopefully by now you have some ideas in mind to implement (or maybe you've already started) around your home so that you can be rockin' and rollin' with ease. The ideas and hacks in this last chapter are just a miscellaneous assortment covering all different areas of your house and life. Could they have been worked into the other chapters? Probably. They're just a *little* bit different though – so now that you have a better idea of changes you're wanting to make in your home, why not have some fun with a few rapid-fire tips that might spark an idea for just the solution you've been looking for? Here we go…

- Try keeping morning and nighttime vitamins wherever you get dressed/undressed each day (for me, it's in my closet), along with a bottle of water (or a cup for water from the sink). This makes it easy to take them at the right time without forgetting!
- Store extra sheet sets inside their pillowcase – this keeps an entire set together, plus makes them easier to stack & store! Also, consider storing extra sheets in the closet of the room that has that size bed in it (rather than a hallway or bathroom "linen closet"). If someone gets sick or has an accident at night, the spare sheets are right there in the

room rather than you having to go dig them out in another part of the house.

- If you have something you need to remember to take with you when you leave the next day, but it must stay in a certain spot until then (such as something in the refrigerator), put your keys with it – then you literally can't leave home without it.

- Keep an empty laundry hamper (the wide, shallow kind) in the back/trunk of your car – then you can fill it with groceries or other items that need to be brought inside. Carry the hamper inside, unload, and then immediately go stick the empty hamper back in your car. This saves you from making multiple trips and makes an easy way to corral items so they're not rolling around in the back of your car too! (I actually use a giant tote from the laundry section at Walmart.)

- Keep a cardboard box somewhere that's out of the way but easy to access (maybe inside a kid's closet or a hallway closet) and mark it DONATIONS. Now any time you have a shirt that no longer fits someone or an item you're no longer going to need, you can easily throw it straight into the donation box (rather than having it somehow end up back in the dirty laundry just to repeat the cycle). Once the box is close to full, simply go set it in the back of your car and you'll be ready to drop it off next time you're out. No more having to spend time going through all the kids' clothes to remind yourself which items were getting too small or trying to gather up little piles you were making of stuff to get rid of. Do you have an older kid whose clothes get passed down to a younger one, but there's an age/size gap in between? Keep a basket in the top of the older one's closet; when there's an item they've outgrown that is still too big for the younger one, toss it in! When that season comes around the next year, pull down the bin and add what fits now to the younger kiddo's clothes.

- Never say "I'll just get gas in the morning." Let's be real – we all know that mornings often don't go as planned! Just go get it now. Speaking of gasoline, also try to never let your tank get below ¼ full as it causes more wear on your fuel pump and other essential parts. (The more you know, right?)
- Consider going back to using a "regular" alarm clock and leave your phone in the kitchen! Or at least leave the phone inside a nightstand drawer, as a backup. This will help combat the urge to scroll on your phone for "just a few minutes" when you get in bed or when you first get up.
- Try setting up a "dinner co-op" with other nearby moms. If there's five of you, each choose 2 recipes (and discuss the meals beforehand so that no one picks the same things) and make 5 batches of each recipe (enough for

each mom to have one). Remember all the tips about how it's cheaper and faster to double/triple/etc. a recipe once you're already making it? This means each mom gets 10 different meals for her family and only had to cook 2 of them! Everyone saved time and money, and you might even discover some new family favorites to add to your collection!

- Got an Amazon delivery? Before you toss the empty cardboard box into the trash or recycling, take five minutes to walk around your house and toss anything you can find to get rid of in the box – random trash someone didn't throw away, the junk mail you just got in the mail, that broken toy that you know you're not really going to fix, etc. Then go toss it all away together. BOOM! You just decluttered some items from your home without even really having to try!

- Grated parmesan cheese lids fit mason jars. You're welcome.

- Consider whether your home/family situation would make it worthwhile to invest in a hot/cold water dispenser for children to be able to use. For large families in particular, this can be a great time and distraction saver (for parents) since it makes it easier for the kids to be able to independently get cold water to drink and have hot water available for mixing oatmeal, instant soup, etc.

- Some tips involve trading extra time to save money, but this one is the reverse. Hate to dust? Spend the extra money to buy high quality air filters for your air-conditioning system, so that more dust particles are trapped by the filter and not distributed around the house through the air vents. (Just don't forget to change the filter at least once a month!)
- If your utility bills are killing your budget, see if you have any extra power/plug strips at home. If so, use these wherever you can to plug in items that don't need to stay turned on all the time. Many items (televisions, small appliances, microwaves, etc.) use up more electricity than you would think just by being plugged in even when they're not in use! Any item in your home that has a clock (coffeemaker, microwave) or remote (TV) is using electricity 24/7. Having them plugged into power strips with a switch that stays at "off" when you're not using something will help reduce the amount of electricity your home uses while "idle", and thus reduce your utility bill. Always be sure to check that it's safe to plug in the item you're considering into a power strip though, so as not to create a risk of fire hazard. You can also simply unplug those items when they're not in use. While it may take you an extra second or two to have to plug in the coffee pot, microwave, or whatever when you're wanting to use

it, the extra seconds can be well worth the money you'll save on your electric bill.

- Random car hack: if you have a spot (like a particular cup holder) where you often drop small items (coins, paper clips, etc.) throughout the week and it tends to get grimy, put a silicone muffin cup in it! Then when it's dirty, you can easily pull the silicone cup out and give it a quick wash before putting it back. This also makes it easy to gather loose change that's been tossed in there, rather than having to dig around with your fingernails to get the last few coins.
- If you go somewhere where you have to park in a multi-level parking garage or an enormous parking lot, snap a pic with your phone of your car and some identifying details (a sign showing what section that is, spot number, or something else easily identifiable). This way you don't have to worry about whether you remember the correct parking section or row when you come back to find your car. Or, set a pin in the gps app on your phone for the location of your parked car.
- Try toothpaste to get dull car headlights clear and shiny again.
- A plastic cereal container with a grocery sack inside makes a great car trash can (and saves you from having to figure out what to do with the sticky item that your kid just handed you as you're going down the highway).

- Keep several large carabiners in your vehicle – they're great to clip to a seatbelt or headrest bar and keep grocery sacks, shopping bags, purses, umbrellas, etc. from falling to the floorboards or rolling around in the seat of your car.
- You've probably heard before that you shouldn't go grocery shopping when you're hungry (which is very true). What you *also* shouldn't do is go shopping (in person or online) just because you're stressed or upset. Spending money to try to temporarily make yourself feel better will only result in you feeling worse and guilty once the brief "high" goes away and you realize you wasted money. Plus, if your budget is tight, you'll just cause extra stress later for Future You by having made things even tighter.
- If you paint a wall, write the brand, color name and finish on the inside of a switch plate or outlet cover in that room. (I suggest the switch plate for the main light in the room.) Now you won't have to worry about forgetting years down the road what color it was if you need to touch up or want to use the same color elsewhere.
- Use the note app on your phone to make a packing list the next time you're going on a trip. The note app on an iPhone will let you put bubbles next to items which can be checked off and unchecked. Make your list and check off items as you pack them. When you are packing to head back home, uncheck the items as you pack them

back into your suitcase. Not only can you make sure nothing gets left behind, but now you have a working packing list saved in your phone for next time so that you don't have to think of everything from scratch again! (If you thought of anything while on your trip that you didn't bring and wish you had, go ahead and add it to the list so you won't forget next time.)

CONCLUSION:

I'm so happy that you stuck with me, friend. I truly hope that you've had some "Aha!" moments, been inspired and found some insight into how you can make simple changes that will ease your stress, overwhelm and the general chaos that us moms have to function in. Remember, this is all about making your life work for you, so take what's relevant and useful to YOU and implement it – and then leave the rest! No routine, habit, or tip is truly "one size fits all." We're using the "throw spaghetti at the wall" theory, remember? See what sticks for you. I don't care what changes you make or how you run your life – only that you're happy and as stress-free as possible.

Repeat after me: I am amazing. I'm a wonderful, loving mother who is determined to lead by example to teach my kids healthy, productive habits as they grow up. I'm human and make mistakes, and this is important for them to see too! I am focused on progress, not perfection – and I am worthy and deserving of having a fulfilling life that I enjoy.

Nobody is "killing it" all the time. Nobody.

Figure out where your stress points are (the tasks or areas that bother you or stress you out the most) and start your focus there. Is it the chaos of weekday mornings? Then jot down the tips you're most excited to implement to help your morning routine and start with those. Is cooking every night what you dread the most during the week? Then start with some of the meal-planning and cooking strategies mentioned. Do what's needed to improve the most out-of-balance areas in your home and life first. Then once you're feeling more victorious and in control of those, move on to some other aspects of your home!

Keep in mind too that what works for you right now may not be what you need later on down the road. Sometimes you must decide what's more important to you for the phase of life that you're in at the moment. Is it saving money? Then you need to focus on the tips that save you money and help ease your budget, even if it means you have to spend some extra time and effort to accomplish this. Is saving time in your day what you need most right now? Then focus on routines, habits and "hacks" that will save you time and streamline your life, even if you may pay a little more for the convenience. Are you trying to balance saving time AND money (a true test of sanity)? See which tips speak to you the most and start with those. Perhaps you'll find that you need to devote the time needed to meal plan, batch/pantry cook and watch grocery sale ads because your grocery budget is where you can (and need to) save the most money; and in turn, you can focus on time-saving tips in other areas of your life and home so that things still balance well. What will serve you best right NOW may change later – and that's okay! Keep this book handy and when you realize that your daily circumstances have changed you can refer back to certain chapters for ideas on tweaking things a little differently.

No one (especially not me) knows what's right for your family more than you do. Pick and choose the ideas that will help the most for your circumstances and your family to make things easier, simpler, and ultimately happier for everyone.

If you're feeling super inspired and are filled to the brim with ideas of how you're going to revitalize your daily routines and your home, awesome!! Establish some "baby steps" first though and remember to give yourself grace along the way. Establishing new habits takes time! Decide what your "baseline" will be. What step can you do no matter what? (exercise/walk for 2 minutes; tidy up for 2 minutes; etc.) Something is always better than nothing. Start with a small change or habit that you can easily do no matter what, and make sure you DO IT no matter what. Some days, you'll feel energized by the momentum you've started and you'll go further/longer. Great! Some days you won't want to do anything and doing that tiny 2-minute habit may seem silly and pointless - but you're still going to do it (no matter what), and if that's literally all you change for that day then that's good enough. Making progress in adding in new routines or habits requires rewiring your brain, and that takes time and consistent repetition. So just keep going with the "something is better than nothing" habit until you don't even have to think about it anymore and you just do it on autopilot – then you can start to add more to it.

Be willing to be "not great" at it! Progress means that you're not going to be amazing at something right out of the gate. But if you want to ever be better at it, you have to just get started and go from there. Would you suggest you're your kid quit baseball just because they didn't hit a home run their first week? Of course not. So why do we tend to set such high, unobtainable standards for ourselves when we're the ones trying to make a change? Remember, a Simple SuperMom isn't perfect! She's just willing to put some effort into setting herself up for success and making it easier for her to be her best self. YOU are going to be a great Simple SuperMom – I just know it!

One of the most important things that I hope you take away from this book is that YOU deserve the same care that you would give your children. Often as mothers we focus so much on taking care of everyone else – making sure the kids eat nutritious healthy food, take their vitamins, get a bath each day, etc. – that we fail to leave room to care for ourselves as well. You deserve all those same things too! This applies to every woman – whether you're a mother or not – you deserve to treat yourself well! Self-care is not just a popular catch phrase. It is a real, vital part of caring for your own mental and physical well-being, and it serves those around you just as much as it serves yourself. Now, am I saying that you should abandon all housecleaning, cooking, and paying bills in favor of binge-watching Netflix and eating an entire package of your favorite cookies? No, because *that isn't self-care*! Don't get me wrong – we all have times where we need to just stop, let go of any remaining responsibilities for the day, and give ourselves some time to decompress, relax, or even forget.

But doing that on the regular isn't self-care, it's self-sabotage. Acknowledge when you truly do physically or mentally need a break, but don't swing too far the other way and make things worse and more stressful for yourself in the long run by ignoring tasks that need to be addressed. Meal-planning and batch-cooking are just as much valid forms of self-care for me as long soaks in my tub while watching YouTube or going out to dinner with some girlfriends. Care for Current You and help her care for Future You – because ALL of you deserves to live a life that you love, without losing too much of your time, money, or sanity in the process!

Do your best and it will be enough.

All my love to you, friends!

Made in the USA
Las Vegas, NV
19 November 2022